Highly Effective Lean Teams

Highly Effective Lean Teams

By

Ronald L. Buckley
Candace Lynn Buckley

Shady Brook Press
Norwalk, CT

Highly Effective Lean Teams
Copyright © 2012
By Ronald L. Buckley

All rights reserved

ISBN-13: 978-1480286900

ISBN-10: 1480286907

Cover Design by:
Hillary Barron, Graphic Designer

Photograph:
Spencer Barron
Claudia Barron
Candace Buckley
Christopher Buckley

Except for brief quotes used in reviews, no part of this book may be reproduced by any means without the written permission of the Author.

Published by
Shady Brook Press
14 Shady Brook Lane
Norwalk, CT 06854

Other Books by the Author

Winning in a Highly Competitive
Manufacturing Environment
Ronald L. Buckley

No Eraser Needed
Mistake Proofing Your Business
Ronald L. and Candace Lynn Buckley

My Toaster's Grandfather
A Simple Look at Lean Operations from a
Toaster's Point of View – One Slice at a Time
Ronald and Lucinda Buckley

Winning Manufacturing Solutions
Optimizing Performance
With Lean Strategies
Ronald Buckley
Lucinda Buckley

Lean Business Drivers
Ronald L. Buckley
Lucinda A. Buckley

DEDICATION and ACKNOWLEDGMENT

I dedicate this effort to the marvelous men and women I have had the great privilege of working with over the last thirty plus years. I also acknowledge their contribution to this work. I profoundly hope that this book conveys the tremendous respect and gratitude I have for these people and their efforts.

Contents

Chapter 1 –   15
    Introduction

Chapter 2 –   23
    What Does It Mean to Be Lean?

Chapter 3 –   33
    Self-Directed Cross-Functional Teams

Chapter 4 –   65
    Mistake-Proofing Teams

Chapter 5 –   117
    The Workout Team Process

Chapter 6 –   127
    Problem-Solving Tools and Techniques

Chapter 7 –   141
    Team Dynamics

Epilogue   155

Chapter 1

Chapter 1

Introduction

In this book I will use simple and direct language to describe a step-by-step process that can be used to improve the way you run your organization through the use of Teams. Specifically, I will describe three types of Teams that I have found very effective in my businesses. They are the Self-Directed Cross-Functional Team, the Mistake-Proofing Team, and the Workout Team. Each type of Team is unique, but all have common characteristics:

- All the Teams build an incredible amount of effectiveness by sharing ideas among and between Team members.

- All three types of Teams use similar problem-solving tools, which I will cover in a later chapter.

- All three types improve communications. Communications between individuals and organizations can't help but be improved when fellow employees sit next to one another working on a common goal.

- The Teams are cross functional, some by design, others by their nature.

- These Teams will change the culture of your organization by getting the people closest to the issues involved in continually improving your business, no matter what your business is.

- These processes will work in virtually any business.

In addition:

- I will use real life examples, which are easy to relate to, to show how successful these Teams can really be.

- I will explore the idea that using these three Team concepts is rewarding, not only as a means to becoming a more efficient organization, but also as a means to achieve great personal satisfaction. You will be involving your employees by unlocking a powerful resource of knowledge and skills and at the same time providing real job satisfaction and security within their own abilities.

- I talk about the progress that can be made through the use of these Teams.

- I will detail how these Teams can be structured for success and made even more potent by making them Cross Functional.

- The Team's accomplishments will leave members with the self-confidence that contributes so much toward creating a workforce that is secure and happy in their work. Happy employees look forward to coming to work. They not only show up regularly, but also are continually striving to improve the Company's competitive position.

Employee involvement is no longer a luxury reserved for corporate giants; it is a necessity for all organizations of any size that intend to thrive. If an organization is going to be successful in the future, it must use and optimize all the productive resources at its disposal—this includes all its employees' talents through employee involvement in a proactive manner at all levels. The Cross-Functional Team is one way to win at the competition game. Invest in, train, and engage all your people. Employees will get involved in a proactive way if they believe they share in and are part of what is going on in your organization. They hunger to be part of the scene and will respond when treated well and like adults, who can deal with the realities that affect their jobs.

The process of coming to the realization that change is necessary to a Company's survival is frustrating. Others in the organization will still be resistant to change. Management support is essential to the success of any major change in the way an organization functions. Consultants can help and sometimes are necessary if only to convince others in the organization that Management is serious. Great care should be exercised when selecting the right consulting firm to help.

I can't express the delight I experienced with the implementation of these Teams. To see employees at all levels, some with less than a high school education, putting together presentations for top Management on their own time after hours and then carrying them off in such a sincere and professional manner is a wonderful experience. These employee involvement Teams have been the most incredibly beautiful parts of my career. Once you get a taste of this kind of working environment, you need more; it is addictive in the most positive way. What is possible? Just about anything your employees put their minds to. Your people are the best chance your Company has to succeed at beating the competition.

There is really nothing very complicated here, just simple concepts and ideas. These are things every Manager owes himself or herself and his or her people: continuous improvement through training and education, open and honest up-front communications, and employee involvement in a Team atmosphere.

Chapter 2

Chapter 2

What Does It Mean to Be Lean?

What is *Lean*? "*Lean* is a system of process improvement designed to eliminate waste through the application of lean practices and tools optimizing value with the most efficient use of capital, equipment, and materials." *Capital* includes your people and their talents, *equipment* includes your business systems, and *material* includes all the material you use in the process of satisfying your Customers' requirements. *Lean* lowers costs, greatly improves competitive advantage, is applicable to all types of businesses, and creates a cultural transformation in your business.

In today's fast-paced, rapidly changing business environment, companies can no longer just count on the Business Leader or even the

Leadership Team to manage the business. You must involve all your employees in the success of your Company. Your van driver is no longer just a driver. He or she must come to work every day seeking better ways to do his or her job. All employees must be aware of the processes they use to execute their duties and continually be searching for ways to do their jobs better—error free. Continually improve or perish.

Consumers are in the driver's seat. They want the highest quality at the lowest possible cost, and they want it when they want it—when they want it, not when you promise it, but when they want it. Gone are the days when it was enough to deliver just when you promise to. If your promise does not coincide with your customer's desire, he will consider you late, even if you deliver when promised. If you can't satisfy your Customer, soon someone else will.

Relationships with Customers and Clients are no longer enough to keep the business. Your Customers are under that same pressure you are. They will be forced to seek the price, quality, and service they need, regardless of your long-standing relationships. When a better deal comes along, they will be forced to take it. You and your Customers will be forced to "take the better deal" by shrinking profits, global competition and in some cases, an oversupply of product and services—the general commoditization of just about everything.

Product life and profitability cycles are shortening. Look at the smartphone introduced a few years ago and originally dominated by one player. Now there are several players, and a few who could not keep up have already been dismissed. Even the players left standing have to introduce an updated version every few months just to maintain their superior position. Life cycles that used to be five to ten years have been reduced to months in some cases. Digitization has ushered in a new era of hypercompetition.

Intellectual property is under pressure and does not offer the protection it once did. Smaller businesses are at a disadvantage when defending their patents and other forms of intellectual property. Large companies can afford to spend millions on legal fees, whereas smaller companies can't bear the expense of defending their positions. Add to this the shortening lifecycles of products caused by rapid advances in technology, and intellectual property protection becomes greatly minimized.

So where does all this leave us? It leaves us in a situation where it is very difficult for most companies to pass cost increases on to their Customers. Customers will just look elsewhere—they will be forced to by their circumstances. They will not be able to just pay and then pass on the cost. If they are the end user, they will not be willing to pay more for the same value they can get elsewhere. Consumers recognize that there is only so much to go around in an environment where incomes and net worth have been shrinking—not to mention concerns about deflation and inflation.

The Need to Create a Very Efficient Money-Making Organization

You must create a very efficient money-making organization to survive. This means you must be able to compete with the best of companies. You do this by becoming a "World Class Organization." By that I mean you must be delivering the highest quality services and products at the lowest possible cost when your customer wants them—no sooner or later. Quality, price, and delivery—this is what we all want when we buy goods and services.

To be "World Class" you must optimize all the productive resources at your disposal. Again, the talent—your employees, the equipment—your business systems employed properly and materials that meet or exceed your Customers' requirements. Quality levels should be approaching Six Sigma (3.4 failures per million opportunities) with an ultimate goal of zero defects in everything you do—failures and errors virtually eliminated. Cost reduction becomes part of the culture—credits and refunds must be kept near zero. The Company must keep Customer commitments all the time, which includes delivering when your Customer wants you to. This is where you must be.

To do this we have to accept and get all our employees to accept the following. The key responsibilities of **ALL employees,** not just the Leaders in your business, must be to:

- Generate profits for our investors—if we don't generate profits, how will we stay in business? Everyone involved in the business must clearly understand this. It always amazes me how many people are surprised when I tell them the primary goal of the for-profit business that employs them is to make money.

- Provide a healthy, happy work environment for the employees. I usually never get an argument with this one.

- Perpetuate the Business. This not only encompasses paying your taxes, obeying the laws, getting the proper permits, being a good corporate citizen, etc., but also includes reinventing the business when necessary. For many companies this is a cultural transformation that involves getting everyone to sign up and participate in making the business the best that it can possibly be. And I do mean every employee and stakeholder no matter what they do for the business.

The Teams described in the pages that follow will clearly show you how to get all stakeholders involved in making your business successful—a very efficient money-making organization.

Team Motivation and Empowerment

Team motivation and empowerment starts with setting expectations. There is magic in a quantified objective. If you tell a Team of employees to go off and save me some money on purchase costs, you will get one reaction and quite another if you tell that Team to go off and save 20 percent or $10,000,000 on purchase costs. In addition to empowering your people, a stretch goal forces people to think differently about how they approach achieving a goal. In this example, telling your sourcing people to go off and save some money will probably result in them squeezing vendors in price negotiations; however, telling them to save 20 percent will force them to expand their thinking to include other people in other areas of the business in finding ways to save money by asking, *What do I do outside that I should bring inside*? or *What do*

I do inside that I should take outside? or *How can I save on overhead costs if I do this or that?* They will see the value in a Cross-Functional Team to achieve their goals.

Chapter 3

Chapter 3

Self-Directed Cross-Functional Teams

For those initiatives that are too big in scope or that would take too long to accomplish using the Mistake-Proofing Teams described in the next chapter, you should use the Self-Directed Cross-Functional Team. Use the talent you already have in place to meet your big challenges by setting stretch goals and by making the Teams cross functional to draw on the various talents across the organization.

Having a Team that crosses functional lines is expedient in that it will make available the diversity of talent usually required to address the initiatives that touch more than one area of the business. Another benefit derived from forming a Cross-Functional Team is the team's ability to eliminate resistance and break down barriers at the grassroots level. By including as Team members individuals who are respected by their peers, the Team's ideas will be more readily accepted—the Team sells their ideas to the employees they interface with routinely. It may even be a good idea to include an individual on the Team who is believed to be resistant to this type of change. Eliminating resistance through Team membership is an excellent way to create a convert, and converts will become the project zealots. Another good reason for forming a Cross-Functional Team is that, when one of the Team members works in a given area of the business, the Team can more easily draw on resources from that area. For instance, Information Technology assistance is easier to secure if the person asking for the assistance is an employee from the Information Technology end of the business.

     In addition to being Cross Functional the Team is Self-Directed. *Self-Directed* means just that, Self-Directed. Most of us cannot rely on ourselves alone to accomplish major initiatives. It is usually necessary to draw on the talents of the people around us. The Team concept is far more effective without a dominating personality being present. Optimum Team performance is fostered when all Team members participate equally in the Team process. When all Team members feel that their ideas are important, they will give them freely. The senior member of Management forming the Team should pick the Team Leader, Team Facilitator, and then—together with these individuals—pick a few candidates for Team membership. At the first Team meeting after the Team has been formed, the senior Manager forming the Team will address the Team to deliver the challenge.

After the Team challenge has been delivered, this individual leaves the Team meeting, not to return unless invited by the Team. Great care must be used by Management not to interfere with the Self-Directed Team's work. This may even mean biting one's tongue and accepting what you believe to be mistakes in the interest of noninterference. Once an outsider with the power to interfere and usurp the Team's authority does so, you no longer have a Self-Directed Team. If things are so bad that interference is absolutely necessary, request an invitation to address the Team and lay out your concerns. Make the Team understand that they are the decision makers. Your guest appearance is just to make suggestions the Team may elect to ignore. If your guest appearance fails to gain the desired results and greater interference is warranted, disband the Team and start over. Using your influence at this point will neuter the Team anyway, so just start over with a fresh Team. Remember—responsibility, accountability, and authority go together; you can't have one without the other two. A policy of noninterference will make your Self-Directed Teams a powerful force in your business.

One of my actual experiences with a Self-Directed Cross-Functional Team that didn't take my advice led me to allow the Team to spend a few thousand dollars more than they had to. Okay, I'll say it—waste a few thousand dollars. The Team, when in the process of setting up a new data-collection system, insisted on installing too many barcode readers and printers. The Team wanted to place a reader and printer at the birthing station. This is the station that adds the initial barcode to an item, giving it identity, and starts the clock ticking for the cycle time measurements. The Team also wanted barcode readers at five other stations in the process. I requested and was granted an audience with the Team. I expressed my concern, telling the Team that when this area was converted, there would be no need for so many readers because the product would not be in the area long enough. The Team was playing the game under the current rules, by which product remained in the area for weeks, not days or hours. I was drawing on my previous experience, which told me that soon the crippling shortage situation would be cured, and products would no longer take weeks to move through this area; it would take less than two days from the birthing station to the end of the line. I was eventually proven correct, but not before the Team purchased and installed every reader and printer it originally wanted installed. Obviously, the Team was unmoved by my argument that the product would be moving so quickly through the area that the extra equipment would not be needed. They had lived for so many years with the shortage problems that they could not comprehend what life would be like without the shortages—their past experience dictated their actions.

I believe two things were going on in this situation. First, the Team believed that the equipment was needed. Second, the Team was testing to see if Management really meant what it said about the Teams' being Self-Directed. Four different Self-Directed Cross-Functional Teams had been simultaneously kicked off, and this was the first test. If at this early stage of Team empowerment I had overruled the one Team on its decision to purchase the equipment, the success of all the Teams would have been jeopardized. It was far better to spend a few extra dollars making an investment in the Team process than to undermine the Team's authority. Management gave the Teams the responsibility; Management intended to hold the Teams accountable. It was necessary for Management to reaffirm the Teams' authority. All four Teams went on to be very successful, saving the Company millions of dollars. The extra equipment was a good investment.

Influencing the Team

There are several ways for a Team's creator to influence the Team's performance. The first will be through the Team Leader and the Team Facilitator, both of whom the Team's creator appointed when the Team was formed. The Team will generate minutes of each meeting. The minutes will be distributed not only to the Team members, but also to the Team's creator. In this way the Team's creator will know what direction the Team is headed. It is acceptable for the Team creator to attempt to influence both the Team Leader and the Team Facilitator, but not the Team Members. The Facilitator should be skilled in dealing with conflict and have the ability to deal in a professional manner with any conflicts that may arise. The Team's creator, knowing that conflicts may arise between what the Team perceives is in the best interest of the organization and what Management perceives is in the best interest of the organization, should pick the Facilitator carefully.

Another way for Management to influence the Team is to set dates for Team presentations. A very important element contributing to the success of the Self-Directed Cross-Functional Team concept is the Team presentation. The Team should be required to give periodic presentations to a member of the senior Management Team on a regular basis. The stated purpose of the presentation will be to update Management on the Team's progress. The unstated purpose is to keep pressure on the Team to continue to make progress toward meeting the Team challenge. No one wants to get up in front of his or her Management during a presentation and confess that the Team has not made any progress. A great deal of pressure will come from the Teammates themselves to "get stuff done" before the presentation date so that the Team can look good to Management.

If the previous Team-influencing methods are unsuccessful at moving the Team in the desired direction, the Team creator can request an invitation to attend a regular Team meeting or even call a special Team meeting. Either should be a very rare occasion. Too many of these requested audiences and you no longer have a Self-Directed Team. Present your best case to the Team. Make sure they understand that you are not dictating to them, but also make it clear that you are trying to influence their decision. Then, leave the meeting while the Team considers your suggestions.

In addition to the above, you can always count on human nature. There is usually an inclination for the Team to want to please the Team's creator. So make your positions known. Keep the lines of communication between senior Management and the Team open, upfront, and honest. The Team will appreciate Management's giving them free rein in meeting the challenge.

They will be inclined to please. And, of course, all Teams must operate within existing Company policies.

The Nuclear Option

If the Team creator finds that a Team has gone completely off the rails and cannot be brought back into line using the influencing tactics above, there really is only one option left. Disband the Team and start over with a new Team. To go much further than the steps above in influencing a Self-Directed Team would destroy the Self-Directed element so important to the success of these Teams. Therefore, the "nuclear" option of dissolving the Team really is the only choice.

Team Training

Soon after forming any new Team, provide the entire Team with formal Team training. Many human resources leaders have had experience with Team training, but if you have no one who can provide Team training inside your organization, this type of training is readily available through various human resource organizations.

The training should cover the various stages of Team development that most Teams go through, from the kickoff stage through the productive stage. Explaining these stages will help the members understand what to expect in their interactions with their fellow Teammates. Other topics should include the following:

- Why governance is important.

- An overview of what is expected of the Team Leader, the Team Facilitator and the Team Members.

- An explanation of how the Team Leader's role changes as the Team matures. (The Team Leader assumes more of a Team Member's role as the Team matures and leadership is not as necessary as it was when the Team was first formed.)

No role is more important here than the Team Facilitator's role. Unless the Team Facilitator already has relevant experience and training, it would be wise to provide facilitator training to the individual serving in this role. Although a full member of the Team, the Facilitator has a unique role in that his or her first responsibility is to the Team process itself. I usually try to get the Team Facilitators from the Human Resources group. These folks make good Facilitators because they are usually far enough removed from the routine day-to-day activities. Good Team Facilitators recognize that their first responsibility is to monitor the Team process. The closer an individual is to the problem at hand, the more difficult it becomes to monitor the Team process. A trained Facilitator should be able to promote and encourage participation by all Team members, run interference with upper Management, maintain fairness, help create a sense of harmony, keep the Team spirit alive, help settle internal disputes, recommend new Team members, and encourage the celebration of successes.

The Team Challenge

The Team challenge should be easy to understand, measurable, have a time limit, and be relevant to the success of the business. It should be a stretch to achieve, yet achievable. Some actual examples of Team challenges follow:

- Reduce the cost of mistakes by $800,000 over the next twelve months through the use of Mistake-Proofing methods.

- Train every employee on all levels in Mistake-Proofing methodology over the next ninety days.

- Reduce inventory by $10,000,000 by May 1.

- Implement a bar-coding system that tracks all orders from order to receipt by June 1.

Team Governance and Characteristics

Below I have listed a few rules of governance and conduct I have found successful in managing Self-Directed Cross-Functional Teams over the years.

- *Team size should be more than five and less than twelve.*

    With less than five people you sacrifice the benefits of having a Cross-Functional Self-Directed Team. Remember one of the most powerful reasons for having such a Team is to gain acceptance in the affected areas; use too few people and you give up something here. More than twelve Team members and the Team is too unwieldy. There are too many group dynamics going on. It just gets too hard to keep anybody happy.

- *Each Team is composed of a Team Leader—appointed; a Facilitator—appointed; a Secretary to keep minutes—elected; and the Team members—invited or drafted.*

    These positions are those described above. If no one volunteers to take the minutes, the task can be rotated. The Team Leader and Facilitator should review the minutes before they are distributed.

- *The Team should meet at least once a week.*

  Making this a ground rule forces the Team to meet and keep things moving. If the Team is meeting less than once a week, one has to question whether there is really a project going on or not. The first sign of trouble here will show up in the Team minutes (or lack thereof).

- *When a Team accomplishes its goals and the challenge has been met, the Team should be disbanded.*

  The on-going efforts can continue to be supported with the use of a steering committee rather than a Self-Directed Cross-Functional Team. The Teams should be used to define and execute major projects using the unique talents of the Team members. The work is usually over and above the Team members' everyday assignments; however, the challenge should be connected to the everyday work the Team member is normally assigned. In fact, it is best if the Team member will be a beneficiary of the successful Team outcome.

- *The Team must create an infrastructure that will survive the Team effort so that the accomplishments of the Team will continue to bear fruit long after the Team has been disbanded.*

  In fact, the remaining infrastructure should outperform the Team that created it.

- *The Team sets goals and assigns tasks to meet the challenge.*

  The Team creator establishes and delivers the challenge at the first Team meeting. However, the Team sets the goals that will have to be met to satisfy the challenge. In the case of a Self-Directed Team it would be counterproductive and presumptuous for the creator to set the Team's goals. The nature of the ongoing dynamics involved in the Teamwork will dictate changing goals as the Team progresses in its work. It would not be practical to have a Self-Directed Team and have the Team creator set the goals. This would negate the self-direction aspect of the Team.

- *The Team is empowered to draw on the talents and expertise available elsewhere in the Company.*

  This includes the entire organization. The talent would most likely be required on a part-time basis. For example, if help is required from the Sourcing Group to get vendor quotes for posters and promotional materials, a buyer will be assigned to the Team until the quoting is complete. In this case, it would make no sense for the Buyer to become a full Team member for the duration of the Team's existence, so a temporary assignment will serve the Team well. One note here: when the time comes to hand out the rewards for the Team's successes, don't forget to include the part-timers in proportion to their efforts.

- *Team meeting attendance and showing up on time are both important and mandatory in order to maintain Team membership.*

  The Team must establish these ground rules early on, in the first or second meeting. It is a must that all Team members understand the rules. The entire Team must agree to the boundaries. Consequences for noncompliance must be established and adhered to. So many Teams fail to address these difficult issues at the outset, then a member starts missing meetings or letting the Team down in some way and the Team has no recourse. The Team creator should place a strong emphasis on the ground rule setting needs at the kickoff meeting when the challenge is delivered. The Facilitator, especially if he or she is a Human Resource professional, can help with this process.

One Team's actual experience involved a Team member who continually let the Team down. This failure drove the Team to fire the individual from the Team. This individual served on two Teams and eventually the process was repeated with the other Team as well. Not long after being dismissed from the second Team, the individual left the Company. These Teams both went on to become very successful despite this episode. The separation from the Team was handled professionally, partly because the mechanism was in place, having been dealt with at the Team's inception. The ability of the Team to terminate a Team member from the Team can be a powerful motivator. Most people would prefer to be fired by their Company than to be fired by their peers.

- *Teams are expected to give progress reports in the form of a presentation to a senior member of Management, the more senior the better.*

As noted earlier, having to give presentations helps Teams to keep the project on track. It is the ultimate in Team pressure. The peer pressure to be prepared to deliver a good presentation is awesome. Nobody wants to go before top Management unprepared or with little to show for the Team's effort.

This is the Team's opportunity to show off their abilities. They have a captive audience—a chance to get top Management to listen. I have seen wondrous things happen during Team presentations. There is some real give and take that goes on in these meetings. A Team needing additional resources may ask for Management's commitment after trying to convince Management that the Team is worthy of further investment. It is impressive to see the effort that most Teams put into their presentations. They usually surprise—on the upside—with their command of the issues surrounding their project. Some of the presentations are on the light side, and as such create an atmosphere of excitement and fun. Remember every Team member should participate in some fashion.

- *Other governance ground rules should be established at the outset, at the first or second meeting, by the Team.*

    We have already talked quite a bit about the importance of this action. Addressed should be issues like missing meetings without an excuse, being late for meetings regularly, consequences, majority rule, open vote versus closed vote, level of expected effort, procedure for adding members or removing members, frequency of meetings, and any other issues the Team deems necessary to cover. The Team creator should highlight the importance of establishing these ground rules early. He or she should explain that although it is hoped that the mutual respect the Team members have for each other will be enough to resolve any issues that come up, it is good business practice to formalize the ground rules governing Team activities and behavior, if only to avoid any misunderstanding.

Team Celebrations and Awards

Celebrations are a great way to say thanks and encourage more of the same results that will bring more celebrations. Celebrate even the small successes. They can be as simple as a cake and coffee break or a pizza party. The acknowledgment for a job well done is the important thing. Just say thanks. Companies with more resources can do more—cash awards, gift certificates, etc.

In addition to the minor celebrations along the Team's path to meeting the challenge, one of my companies gave each Team member a $1,000 cash award, and the Team Leader received $1,500 for his or her efforts. Yet another Company I was involved with gave each employee a check for $250 each time the Team gave a presentation to top Management. This in no way was meant as compensation for the work they had done. In most cases it would not have amounted to fifty cents an hour in compensation for all the extra hours the Team members put in on the projects. The awards were a way to say thanks for their efforts. It was as much a bonus for their spouses who sacrificed while their husbands or wives worked extra time. On one occasion several members from one Team in Connecticut were asked to spend Valentine's Day in Milwaukee, Wisconsin. The Team Leader had roses sent to the Team members' spouses back in Connecticut. What a hit that was; they talked about that gesture for months. Another Team had the Company cafeteria prepare dinners to be taken home for the spouses of the Team members that had to work late on a project. This cost the Company only a few dollars each and demonstrated to the Team members' families that the Company recognized and was appreciative of the sacrifice the whole family was making in order to help create a stronger, more secure employment situation for all involved. It made the employees look like heroes in their families' eyes.

Some Teams would give away leather binders with the Team name on the cover. Others would have ball caps or jackets. This was a way for the Team members to build Team spirit and identify and be identified with the Team. Evening mystery cruises, dinner theater tickets, baseball tickets—you name it—and these Teams did it. They worked hard and had fun doing it.

Benefits of Self-Directed Cross-Functional Teams

One of the nicest benefits of forming Self-Directed Cross-Functional Teams is their ability to break down traditional barriers between departments. Team members are placed in situations in which they have to rely and depend on one another's talents and skills to succeed as a Team. There is nothing like these types of situations to harvest respect for fellow employees. Just becoming familiar with a coworker's responsibilities and daily challenges brings an understanding between individuals and groups. Development of mutual respect is a natural byproduct of an entire Team drawn from different areas of the business, pulling in the same direction to achieve a common goal.

Improving communication is another Team benefit. Communications between individuals and organizations can't help but be improved when fellow employees sit next to one another working on a common goal. Remember the Team must meet at least once a week.

The Self-Directed Cross-Functional Teams will foster camaraderie, and the goodwill created will far outlast the Teams or their efforts. After all, many have learned a new common lingo through their Teamwork. The friendships and relationships developed through the Teamwork will spill over into the other day-to-day activities in the rest of the business. Some of the relationships between employees even spill over into their personal lives. In some of my companies there were strong personal relationships that continued for years after the Team effort was over. Members joined professional organizations together, and some went to night school together.

Employees develop a sense of ownership when asked to resolve a major issue that deeply affects the Company's success. The project becomes their "baby." They want to see that nothing adverse happens that will negatively affect their baby. And, of course, when a Team member gets close to a project, he or she is getting closer to the entire Company. The more people have invested in a Company, the keener they are about the health of that Company.

We end up with better, longer-lasting improvements that are implemented much more quickly. With limited resources, where does a Company get the talent it needs to run the day-to-day business while at the same time making great improvements on a grand scale? The answer is the "Self-Directed Cross-Functional" Team.

The MAGIC

There is magic in a Self-Directed Team. As a matter of fact, there are three forms of magic:

- First, the Team has the power to fire Team members. That puts great pressure on the Team Members to perform. We all have been on Teams with eight members where three do all the work. That can't happen on a Self-Directed Team. The risk of being fired by your peers is too great.

- The second form of magic is the requirement to make a presentation for top Management. Who wants to tell their top Management that they have been working on a problem for months and haven't accomplished anything?

- The third form is the magic of a quantified objective.

No Work Happens Until the Tool Hits the Material

Use these Teams to get the work done. One thing I remember from my college physics classes—no work happens until the tool hits the material. You get up in the morning, shower, dress, eat breakfast, and drive to your place of work. You may get a cup of coffee, collect your tools, or lay out the work you need to do in front of you. Up to this point, *no work has happened*. Not until you pick up the tool—be it pencil, pen, or screwdriver—and touch it to the material, has any work happened. Once the tool has touched the material, then you can claim that work has happened. Your "Self-Directed Cross-Functional" Teams are your tools. Your challenges are their work. Your job as creator is to bring them together.

Examples of Self-Directed Teams

Reduce inventory by $10,000,000 by the end of the year. This was the challenge of an Inventory Reduction Team. The Team was very successful. They started with $24,000,000 in inventory and successfully reduced that inventory to $14,000,000. In actuality there were three distinct Inventory Teams in this same Company, serving in succession. The three Teams eventually drove inventory down to $7,000,000, while at the same time top line revenue doubled, making the inventory investment work more than six times harder than it had prior to the Teams' work.

The second inventory reduction Team was formed after the first Team was disbanded, and the third Team was formed after the second Team was disbanded. A "Self-Directed Cross-Functional" Team should be disbanded with a celebration when it has met its challenge. If this were not the case, the Teams would go on forever, tying up valuable resources that should be focused elsewhere. Three different Teams were required because, although the goal of reducing inventory was common to all three Teams, the methods they had to use to achieve their goals were quite different. Hence, three different Teams were composed of people with different talents who were able to deal with the different issues facing each of the three Teams. For instance, the first inventory Team focused on issues such as selling used inventory equipment, reworking unusable inventory into usable inventory, then selling it, and returning unneeded material to the vendors who supplied it or pushing off material deliveries by rescheduling Purchase Orders. There were Team members from Sales and Marketing to help move the inventory, as well as members from areas of the business to help figure out how to repair and rework unusable inventory into usable inventory. By the time the last of the three inventory Teams started its work, members were focusing on things like reducing the size of the material Kanbans and integrating assemblies. The makeup of the final Team didn't include any members from Sales or Marketing; its membership centered on the supply chain.

Improve on-time delivery hit rate to the 99 percent+ level over the next year. This Team was coming from so far back that it actually took almost a year and a half to satisfy the challenge. On-time delivery was at 53 percent when the Team challenge was delivered. Also, some of the late orders were weeks late, not just a few days. The Company was shipping more than 10,000 line items a month to virtually every hospital in the United States and many outside the USA. An order was considered on time if it was shipped prior to the promised ship date. No tolerance window was allowed. If the order was one minute late, it was counted as late. Prior to the Team measuring the on-time delivery for the first time, this Company didn't even know how bad its delivery rate was.

The Team's members came from the various areas of the Company that had the most influence over on-time delivery, including Order Entry, Customer Service, Sales, Shipping/Logistics, Sourcing, and Manufacturing, and the Facilitator was the Human Resources Manager. These Team members addressed and improved a variety of issues that were causing late deliveries, such as unrealistic promises to Customers, late vendor deliveries causing late builds, priority setting, freight carrier selection, short shipments, order entry errors, and Customer ordering errors.

When the Team was disbanded, it left behind a strong infrastructure to build on its successes for years to come. Eventually, on-time delivery was defined as the date the Customer requested the delivery at the Customer's site. This is a much tougher method of measuring on-time delivery, basing your performance on the date the Customer wants the delivery, rather than on the date you promised the delivery. When you know you are being measured, you tend to pad the delivery promise. With the new, tougher measure, the Customer can be unreasonable and the measurement stands—meet the request and you are on time; miss the request and you are late. Also, early shipments were not allowed and partial shipments were not allowed.

Improve on-time deliveries from 75 percent to 99 percent over the next five months. This consumer products Company was about to lose its biggest customer for one of its key product lines. The customer, the largest retailer in the United States of America, insists that its suppliers maintain a high degree of on-time delivery. If the shelf space reserved for the products is empty, it could be filled with a competitor's product. The Team put in place Kanban techniques both internally and externally to resolve many of the issues causing the poor performance. Meeting the challenge restored on-time delivery to the 99 percent+ level, saving the customer relationship.

Reduce purchase costs for services and materials by $3,000,000 annualized, over the next ten months. When my partner and I first visited this client to interview the key employees, we were told that the purchase cost savings goal for the next year was $75,000. The annual spend for services and material was $40,000,000—not a very aggressive goal. A few weeks later we started a Self-Directed Team and gave them a challenge of saving $3,000,000 over the next ten months. At first they looked at us like we had two heads, but soon accepted the challenge after being assured the task was very doable. The previous goal of $75,000 did not require much imagination—just some negotiation with their suppliers. The new stretch challenge of $3,000,000 required that they change their approach. Rather than just negotiating with suppliers, Team members had to think about what they made in-house and what they purchased outside and rationalize each decision. In addition they looked at reducing warehouse space, insurance costs, and transportation as well as other costs. The results were amazing. The $3,000,000 challenge was met in six months, not ten. In ten months they had saved $4,000,000 and in one and a half years, they had saved a total of $8,000,000.

Reduce floor space requirements by 50 percent within the next year. This Team actually reduced floor space by more than 50 percent within the year by converting the facility to a pull Kanban system with point-of-use delivery and requiring some partnering with suppliers to deliver directly to customers. These efforts eliminated virtually all warehousing and storage requirements.

Streamline new product introduction process so that 100 percent of new products are introduced on time and within budget in the next eight months. Product introduction was always a challenge for this business as it suffered from short product life cycles. New products made up much of this business' annual revenue. The company seldom introduced product on time and almost never within budget. This Team was so successful that the Company introduced 105 new products on time and within budget the following year.

Relocate the business from Burlington, Massachusetts, to Connecticut in the next sixty days. This Team used the pitcher-catcher approach—the catcher being the group receiving the business in Connecticut and the pitcher being the group moving the business from Massachusetts. Using a Self-Directed Team proved to be an excellent method of managing this move. Not a single customer commitment was missed.

Automate the data collection system— have the new system up and running by January

1. This Team suffered through three different leaders. The first died, the second quit, and the third remained until the Team was disbanded. This Team effort not only suffered through three different Team Leaders, it was a victim of project creep. No sooner was the Team about to wrap up the original project and declare the challenge met, than the parent Company decided to implement a new global ERP system. Of course, this meant that much of the original interface work with the current system had to be done over. It was felt that the Team in place was the closest to the issues and would have the best chance at succeeding with the interface to the new ERP system. Many new requirements were added to the specification to take advantage of the new system's capabilities. The software that the Team had originally selected did not play well with the new system, leading to several ugly work-around solutions. None of these difficulties were the fault of the Team; however, members' spirits were dampened, and the work dragged on with little to celebrate. Eventually the Team delivered on most of the requirements, but it took years—far too long for a "Self-Directed" Team. In retrospect, it would have been far better to sacrifice any benefit derived from the Team's experience with the first iteration of the automated data collection system and start a new Team with the introduction of the global ERP system—a valuable lesson for all involved to remember.

This Team had a very large membership of a dozen members. The specialized knowledge each Team Member had in his or her respective areas dictated the need for a large Team. Also, as this system's effect was far reaching in the organization, the Team's membership was drawn from those many areas most affected in an effort to assure buy in.

One more thought on this Team: the presentations the Team delivered to top Management were superb. Initially the Team had an unbelievable amount of spirit. During one of the presentations delivered to the President of the Company and members of his Staff, the Team did a skit involving every member of the Team. The theme centered on the tons of paper that the Team would be eliminating from the business. They collected one month's worth of paper and filled several carts. Wheeling the carts into the Conference Room drove home the importance of the Team's work. It was a very effective presentation.

Eliminate all obsolete part numbers in the system within the next six months. This was the challenge of the "Part Number Elimination Team." This Team's job was to clean up the part number system that had been in effect for several decades by eliminating part numbers that were no longer needed because they were obsolete or in some cases duplicates. One characteristic that stood out with this Team was its *zeal*. The Team would routinely work through lunch, performing the tedious tasks of investigating each part number that was a candidate for elimination. They would order pizzas and eat while they worked on their own time.

Chapter 4

Chapter 4

Mistake-Proofing Teams

In this chapter I will use simple language to describe a step-by-step process that can be used to help create a very efficient, error-free organization that will better be able to compete with the best of companies through the use of Mistake-Proofing Teams. To make a sometimes dull topic interesting, I will draw on my many years of past business and consulting experiences to share my real life challenges in describing situations that everyone can relate to.

I will explore the idea that implementing a Mistake-Proofing program using Teams to execute is rewarding not only as a means to improve profits but also as a means to achieve great personal satisfaction by developing your employees' knowledge and skills, while at the same time providing real job security within their own abilities. And as we know, happy employees look forward to coming to work. They not only show up regularly, but also are continually striving to improve the Company's competitive position.

What we want to do is turn on each and every Team member's reticular activating device. Okay, this is as complicated as this process gets. Let's say you want to buy a new car and you drive to a nearby car dealer and test drive a beautiful new Ford Explorer (or another type of car you really like a lot). You start to negotiate with the salesman but leave without the car. On your way home, you will see more Ford Explorers than you have ever seen on that road before. Why? Your reticular activating device kicked in. You were sensitized to the sight of Ford Explorers. That's what we want to do to your employees—sensitize them to seeing opportunities in the processes that they use every day to do their work. Just about everything we do we do with a process, but we seldom examine that process to see what we can do to make it a better process. With the right skills, we can.

Introduction to Mistake Proofing Your Business with Mistake-Proofing Teams

Mistake Proofing was perfected to an art form by the Japanese in their manufacturing processes. I had the great privilege of learning directly from the artist himself, Shigeo Shingo. He came to Yale University at the age of seventy-nine to give back some ideas. He said that he had taken the idea of Henry Ford's production line and the American grocery store from America to Japan so he was now giving his Mistake-Proofing ideas to America. He called it Poka-yoke—a close direct translation is "fool proofing." The intent is to minimize the possibility of a worker error through the use of warnings or to eliminate completely worker errors through the "fool proofing" of processes, making work virtually error free. Mistake Proofing is based primarily on simple technology that can be easily grasped by virtually anyone. By applying common sense solutions that seek to permanently fix everyday problems that arise in the workplace, processes become free of errors, making expensive inspections and checks unnecessary and eliminating costly do-overs and rework. Even 100 percent inspection will not catch all the defects. When mistakes are made repeatedly, look to the process for the solution, not to the operator or person performing the task. Everyone makes mistakes, and there are hundreds of reasons for this. Fatigue, boredom, distractions, poor designs, material problems, equipment problems, difficult working conditions, and personal illness are just a few of them. Very few, if any, workers get up and come to work in the morning with the intention of making as many mistakes as possible that day. Nobody really wants to make mistakes. Once this simple premise is accepted, looking to the processes or designs for solutions to problems is easy. The process design may be a good one that works well; however, maybe it can be improved by changing the design just a little to make it easier to execute. This is not to say the design is poor, but only that it can be improved.

Today, the advantages of using Mistake-Proofing Teams has migrated to virtually every area of business: the factory, information technology, accounts payable, accounts receivable, human resources, sales, marketing, distribution, and other so-called backroom groups. Also, I have used these techniques to improve all types of businesses, including manufacturing, construction, health clubs, not-for-profits, accounting firms, records management businesses, engineering firms, retail businesses, and distributors as well as many others. This effort combined with e-business efforts seeks to build a very efficient organization, starting with the process of selling and progressing through the entire business to delivery of products and services. This change has been brought about by the recognition that a process is a process, whether the process is one that is used on the factory floor or a process that is used in an office environment, and it can be enhanced and Mistake Proofed to reduce the possibility of making errors or eliminating the possibility of making errors altogether. Cross-Functional Teams are especially effective because others not so familiar with a particular process can easily see areas of improvement that those regularly involved in may miss or step over. "The longer you are in the presence of a problem, the less likely you are to resolve it." – Maurice Nicol

One of the most powerful characteristics of using Mistake-Proofing Teams is that everyone in your business can participate. All of us have the natural skill that it takes to be a mistake-proofing expert to one degree or another. All that is required is a little training. The training is not expensive and does not require specialized skills to conduct. In fact, the training is more awareness oriented than anything else. Pick someone with a reasonable amount of common sense in the organization and send him or her off to a seminar to become a trainer on the subject or kick-start the initiative by bringing in an experienced trainer to train three Teams of five folks—fifteen people or so—in a two-day session. You may even choose to do both or you may hire an experienced trainer and then select an in-house trainer from the first group of fifteen employees you train. You can use this chapter as a guide and develop your own Mistake-Proofing Teams by closely adopting the precepts herein. Again pick someone with good common sense who wants the job and is well respected by others in the organization. When the training method has been selected and the trainer is in place, train every Team. The more employees looking for ways to permanently eliminate errors, the quicker the organization will arrive at an error-free environment or, at the very least, close to an error-free environment.

   The training should be formal in that it is scheduled and mandatory, yet it should be kept informal in that everyone should be encouraged to participate in the training activity. Pure and simple, make this a condition of employment. New employees should be scheduled to take the course as part of their orientation. If new employees are hired infrequently, the new employee training can be postponed until enough students are available. However, a company shouldn't put off training the new employees too long. If new employee contributions are to be maximized, train them early; a fresh set of eyes can see opportunities that have been missed by your current employees. Remember, according to Maurice Nicol, "The longer you are in the presence of a problem the less likely you are to solve it."

Prerequisite: Changing the Way You View Mistakes in Your Organization

Changing the way you view mistakes in your organization is a prerequisite to acceptance of any Mistake-Proofing program. Your employees, the ones who actually use and execute the processes you will be Mistake Proofing, must believe and accept that mistakes are not purposefully caused by their coworkers, subordinates, or those higher up in the organization. It must be accepted by all that no one gets up in the morning and says, "I am going to work today to make all the mistakes I can." Oh sure, there could be an exception to this rule; however, I have never encountered one in the thousands of employees that I have worked with, and I don't ever expect to. Once you accept this premise, then it is easy to move on to eliminating errors by looking at the process itself or external influences on the process, such as defective materials, tools, methods, or the environment. As long as you focus on placing blame on the individual for mistakes that occur, you will never really eliminate them from your business with your Teams. Therefore, when you find an error that appears to have been caused by an individual, your Mistake-Proofing Teams can take a closer look at the process to find the real cause behind the error and then apply the tools presented in this chapter to prevent the error from ever occurring again.

Examples of Mistake Proofing

As part of the course, each student will be called upon to draw on his or her own life experiences. As mentioned earlier, everyone has had many encounters with examples of Mistake Proofing. Some examples are listed as follows:

- Childproof locks in the home and car
- Circuit breakers
- Refrigerator lights that automatically go out when the door is closed
- Automatic seat belts
- Smoke alarms that beep when the battery is low
- Three-pronged plugs
- Printers that signal low ink levels
- Automatic lights that come on after dark
- Electric eyes on doors
- Grocery store scanners
- Self-cleaning ovens that lock when cleaning
- Cameras that will not allow a picture to be taken if the lens cover is not removed

In addition to the common Mistake-Proofing methods we all encounter, many examples can be found in the workplace. Some examples are listed below:

- Double switches on machinery that require both hands be occupied so that a hand cannot be placed in harm's way when the machine is operating

- Software that requires an operator check before deleting data

- Software that requires one to fill in missing data to complete an application

- Spreadsheets with built-in cross footing that double checks the accountant's totals

- Barcode scanners that eliminate keying errors all too common in keyboard entry

- Relationship databases—these databases compare an actual set of data to a stored, predetermined set of desired data that should be achieved under the given circumstances

- Photo sensors that detect the presence of an object

- Automatic on/off timers

- Notched parts that can fit only one way (e.g., three-pronged plug)

- Shaped parts that match the same shape receptacle, allowing only one orientation on contact (e.g., USB port and stick)

- Color-coded paper sets that make sure the customer takes the correct copy

- Test equipment that senses dip switch settings and will not allow the process to continue until the desired settings are present

- Circuit board in-circuit testers that exercise the circuit and can check for shorts (opens), component orientation, component presence, and component values

- Scales that check counts

- Interlocked doors that cannot be opened when another door is open (e.g., in a darkroom where double doors are used to keep out light, when one door is opened, the other door is automatically locked)

- Templates that prevent picking the wrong parts for a specific order/product—the template covers the bins of parts not needed and only allows access to the components required

- Serial number comparative database that will not allow duplicates—similar to a relationship database—if the number has been used before, it has been stored in the database and cannot be used again.

Levels of Mistake Proofing

There are two levels of Mistake Proofing. The first level (the lower-level) makes it easier to recognize when an error is about to occur or an error has just occurred. An example of Mistake Proofing that makes it easier to recognize when an error is about to occur is the warning buzzer that warns you your keys are about to be left in your car's ignition. Also, word processing software that warns with a dialog box that you are about to take an action that will delete an item or save a new document replacing an existing document. These are based primarily on warning alert signals. An example of Mistake Proofing that makes it easier to recognize that an error has occurred is the tray that contains a pin that was supposed to go into the subassembly that was just passed on to the next manufacturing stage. The container would be empty when the next setup was prepped if the pin had been used on the previous assembly. In this case the operator places just the parts required to build one subassembly prior to starting the assembly process. If any parts remain in the bins after completing the previous subassembly, they will be detected at this, the setup point. It is at this point that it becomes obvious a part has been left out of the previous assembly. These are the least desirable Mistake-Proofing methods in that an error can still occur. The next level is the most desirable.

    The second level (the higher level) of Mistake Proofing, the most desirable, is prevention of an error from occurring. With these methods the process is designed not to allow an error to occur. The process may shut down if an error is about to occur or the design of the Mistake Proofing will simply not permit an error to occur. As one progresses from the lower-levels to the higher levels of Mistake Proofing, the process is less dependent on the operator for error-free performance. An example of these Mistake-Proofing methods is the final test equipment that will not allow the final test to be completed unless the DIP switches are set exactly as the software just downloaded into the final product dictates. Another is the notched component that simply will fit only one way in the mating item (USB port) or the component that will work no matter which way it is inserted. Yet another is a database that will not allow you to enter numbers in an alpha field, assign a serial number that has been previously assigned, or pay a bill with an invoice number that is the same as an invoice number on a bill that has been previously paid for the same account. These types of mistake-proofing solutions permanently resolve your mistake-causing issues by not allowing these mistakes to occur in the first place. Often when a higher level solution is not immediately evident, it makes sense to implement a lower-level solution first that provides a warning that a mistake is about to occur or has occurred, to be followed at a later time by a better solution, higher level, that will not allow a mistake to occur.

An excellent example of this is the test equipment above that will not allow the test to be completed unless the DIP switches are set correctly. The first real-life iteration of this Mistake-Proofing process just presented a picture on the display of how the DIP switches would look if they were set correctly alongside of another picture of the way the DIP switches were actually currently set. The theory was that the test operator, seeing how the switches were supposed to be set next to an image of how they were actually set, would fix the problem. In fact, it cured 99 percent of the problems, but we were after a 100 percent fix. The next higher level of Mistake Proofing—preventing the test from being completed unless the switches were set correctly—came later and was the 100 percent fix we were looking for. The important thing to remember is, when you find a lower-level solution, keep looking for that solution that completely eliminates errors by preventing them altogether.

Tools and Methods of Mistake Proofing

The tools and methods of Mistake Proofing are many and varied. The only limits are the extent of the creative abilities and imaginations of the Team members doing the Mistake Proofing. Cost can also be a limiting factor. However, if one method is too costly, find another less costly method that gets you close to a 100 percent solution. Sometimes the method that is chosen may not be the most desirable, yet may be the only one affordable. Some of the various tools and methods are listed here. This list is by no means intended to be a complete one:

- Barcoding that eliminates keying data

- Motion detectors—checking for movement or presence.

- Contact devices—checking for presence

- The design—shape of the design

- Comparative databases—checking for the equivalent or the nonequivalent

- Software that tests for data with specific characteristics

- Scales—checking for presence, volume, or size.

- Using components as conductors that power equipment
- Counters—checking quantity for presence
- Pass-through holes—checking for size
- Control Charts—allow for control of the process
- Templates—ensure access to correct items
- Photo cells—checking for presence or size, quantity, or quality.
- Colors—simple form identification

The Fun Factor

One of the nicest parts of Mistake Proofing is that it is fun work. No engineering degree is required, only common sense. Everyone can get into the act. The next blockbuster idea can come from anyone. Employees from all levels of the organization and all walks of life get to work together resolving problems. This will lower costs and improve quality; what a great way to apply your Team members' talents and energy.

Mistake Proofing: The Story

The following section is devoted to a selection of real Mistake Proofing examples tackled by

Mistake-Proofing Teams. They are actual accounts of Mistake-Proofing opportunities involving some of America's best companies. I hope you will find some of the circumstances familiar and can correlate some of the solutions found on these pages with opportunities for your Teams in your own companies.

Paying the Same Invoice Over and Over

While working in a New Jersey Company, I was asked to approve a vendor's invoice. As the invoice was already approved by another Company Vice President reporting to me who assured me that the services had been provided, I signed, my signature just being a rubber stamp needed because the invoice amount exceeded the VP's approval limit.

Well, two weeks later, after receiving an e-mail from an irate Controller asking why I had approved an invoice that had just been paid for a second time, I found myself confronting the VP who originally convinced me to sign the invoice for payment approval. After some research, to the embarrassment of all involved, the VP came to me with proof that the bill had not only been approved and paid twice, it had actually been paid three times. The same invoice for the same services had been submitted three times, approved for payment three times, and paid all three times. Of course, the funds were recovered from the vendor in the form of a credit.

A Mistake-Proofing Team was assigned the responsibility of coming up with a solution—how could the Accounts Payable process that would allow the payment of an invoice three times for the same services to the same vendor be Mistake Proofed? Simply write a program that compares and rejects the payment of any invoice with the same invoice number to the same approved vendor for the same amount, and the problem is solved. As it turned out, this was a very easy program for the Information Systems group to write and implement.

The Contest Is Over

A packaging group in a consumer products Company had designed a new package for a marketing campaign that included a postcard size insert offering the contest winner season tickets to all home games of a popular baseball Team. The problem was that the product introduction was delayed by several months after the baseball season had ended. To add insult to injury, the expiration date on the entry form had passed ten years before the forms were printed. The Mistake-Proofing Team's solution: use software that will not allow the creation of dated material after the date selected has passed.

More Packaging Trouble

The packaging design group routinely used the copy-and-paste function of its software to save time in designing a package that was very similar to an existing package. The problem was that both products ended up with the same item number. Some customers were being shipped the wrong product. This Mistake-Proofing Team's fix: use a comparative database that will not allow the same part number to be assigned more than once. This Mistake-Proofing method was also used in Connecticut to prevent using the same serial number more than once on more than one piece of medical equipment. It was important that each piece of equipment have a unique number so the item's entire life history could be traced back to the day the serial number was assigned and forward to the day the item is permanently taken out of service.

How Fresh Is That Fresh Food?

The Management of a chain of pet supply stores with a self-service section complained that the food items were spoiling in the bins before they were purchased. The problem was that store employees were not cycling the older product out first. The product on the bottom of the bin was being buried by the newer product when the bins were refilled. The Mistake-

Proofing Team solution: install gravity-fed bins that are angled so that they can be filled from the back side, allowing the customers access from the front, always ensuring that the oldest product is being taken first.

Turning off the Jacuzzi

Several times during the course of a year, employees supervising children's birthday parties would find it necessary to turn off the Jacuzzi to encourage the youngsters to get out of the pool when the party was over and usually just before the next party was to start. Unfortunately turning off the Jacuzzi also turned off the pool circulators. When the Jacuzzi was turned on again with the same switch that turned it off, this action did not start the pool circulators, which then caused the pool heaters to burn out and upset the chemical balance in the pool, making it necessary to cancel activities in the pool to comply with the state law until the chemical balance was restored. The pool downtime was far more costly than replacing the pool heaters.

The first Mistake-Proofing solution the Team came up with was to train everyone working birthday parties at the pool to start the circulators after they shut down the Jacuzzi. This was a *lower-level* solution. Then, after further discussion, the Team developed an *upper-level* solution: separate the circuitry so that turning off the Jacuzzi does not affect the pool circulators.

Note: some of these solutions seem obvious after they have surfaced, and one could ask why it wasn't obvious earlier. The answer is because we routinely just step over problems, not recognizing that they are fixable. We were not sensitized to identifying and finding solutions to process issues—our Reticular Activating Device was not turned on.

Power Losses Cause Tennis Bubbles to Collapse

When the utility power was lost and the backup generators did not start after normal business hours, the tennis bubbles, which require power to maintain positive pressure would collapse, tearing away from attached buildings and crushing lighting fixtures. Although this was rare, it was very costly when it did occur.

The Mistake-Proofing Team's solution: Have the alarm Company notify employees in the middle of the night when power is lost and the generators do not start. The alarm Company has three numbers to call—one after another until they reach someone close by who can go in and get the generators going before damage is done. This service was added to service already in place with the alarm Company for no extra cost.

Late Starts and Early Quits in the Construction Business

At a construction Company in the Southwest, one of the biggest problems was workers showing up late and leaving early from construction sites. All of these employees had barcoded IDs. My first choice for Mistake Proofing this problem would have been to scan the employees in and out, then only pay them for time worked. However, this was not what the Team of workers wanted to do, and the best solution is usually the one that the employees want to implement—they will make it work if it is their idea. Workers were required to sign two forms during the work day relating to work safety and injury. Their Mistake-Proofing solution was to require the employees to sign one of the forms at the gang box before work begins and another at the end of the day. They had to be present to sign the forms. This solution may not have been as elegant as the barcoding solution; however, it got the Company to the same place with a solution that was the Team's idea, rather than one that was imposed on them.

Construction Foreman Ordering Wrong Materials

Foremen were ordering the wrong material from the ordering catalog, and sometimes two foremen would order the same item.

The Mistake-Proofing Team's solution was to use pictures with barcodes next to them so that they could be ordered by scanning the item in the picture which matches the description. Also the data could be easily collected and duplicate open orders could be detected immediately.

Material Thrown Away on Construction Job Sites

This construction Company had decided several years in the past that it was less expensive to throw away leftover material than bring it back to the yard, sort it, and then store it. This may have been a good decision when it was originally made, but the current Team of employees knew better. As material costs increased and contracts got bigger, the circumstances changed significantly.

The Mistake-Proofing Team did an analysis, and it became clear that it would be very profitable to hire someone to sort and restock the material, saving the Company many thousands of dollars a year.

Time Wasted at a Records Storage Company

Employees charged with the responsibility of retrieving files from records storage boxes in a warehouse containing several million boxes of records did not always have enough ladders or flashlights available. There were always plenty of ladders on the first floor but they were a scarce item on the fourth and fifth floors. In addition, there were several areas of the warehouses that were poorly lit, not necessarily because of the poor lighting, but because of the way some boxes were interrupting the light, making finding a specific file inside a specific box difficult. Time lost retrieving ladders and time lost going to the office to get a flashlight was a waste of many labor hours.

The Mistake-Proofing Team's solution was to acquire thirty more ladders and supply each employee with his or her own flashlight. *Again—simple, yet effective solutions seem obvious after the fact. However, these things often go on for years without ever coming up as an issue—issues we just step over. The Mistake-*

Proofing venue is so important in assisting Management in uncovering issues like these.

Infrared Shorts

One of my favorite Mistake-Proofing methods was used by a manufacturer of LEDs and infrared products in Germany. What a surprise I received when, on a visit to this facility as an emissary of a Mistake-Proofing Team, I suggested that just maybe these products were causing some shorts in our products back in the States. This theory of the Team's was dispelled quickly once the owner showed me his manufacturing process. The current that ran his equipment was conducted through the components he was manufacturing for my Company. If the components had a short (open), the equipment would come to a stop. The power would stop once the component with the short reached the final stage in the process for each component where it was conducting the power to run the equipment. Voilà, no more components with shorts ever reached this manufacturer's customers. The Team had to look elsewhere for its solution. It did and discovered that the problem was internal to its processes and easily fixable.

Statistical Process Control (SPC) Leads a Mistake-Proofing Team to Improving Equipment

Imagine a factory floor in Connecticut with thirty shop floor inspectors, just hoping to catch an operator making a mistake to justify their existence. Add to this dozens of processes that could not possibly make a good repeatable product. Then mix these with a labor union grievance process run amok, and you come up with a very nasty, grievance-filled, miserable working environment crying out for a successful Mistake-Proofing program.

The Mistake-Proofing Team found that one area for improvement in this factory was in the cable assembly area. During the introduction of Statistical Process Control (SPC), capability studies were conducted to determine each piece of equipment's ability to manufacture a good quality product on a repeatable basis. Almost every connector-staking machine was found to be unreliable. Either there was a problem with the tooling or the chosen connector for the wire or the calibration of the machine. Cables are not sexy devices, and engineers do not tend to labor over their design; hence, it is an area ripe for finding low-hanging fruit.

The tooling was repaired or replaced. The correct machine was selected for the correct process, and SPC charts were created to monitor the process continually. Reliability and cost were both greatly improved. Prior to this effort, problems were not found until the unit failed the final test. This is the most costly place inside your factory to find defects. Units would fail test (some units went through two hours of testing before failing) and at that point a technician would be required to troubleshoot and repair the unit.

The success of this endeavor, along with similar efforts, increased First-Pass Yield, measured by the number of units that passed test the first time without any rework, from 42 percent to over 99 percent. Although SPC is a great tool in your Mistake-Proofing toolbox, it is not the highest form of Mistake Proofing. Using Statistical Process Control minimizes the possibility of mistakes occurring, but does not completely eliminate the possibility of mistakes happening. Consequently your Mistake-Proofing Teams should use SPC as the first line of defense and continue to look for a higher level Mistake-Proofing solution that will completely eliminate the possibility of an error occurring. One method would be to redesign your product to eliminate the cables through the use of connectors or consolidation of circuits.

By the way, over the next year, all thirty inspector positions were eliminated, and they were replaced through the Mistake-Proofing process by the Teams. Many of the inspectors accepted positions as operators. The ones who wanted to remain inspectors left our employment to haunt other area factories. Not a single grievance was filed in this same factory for years after the last inspector left.

Sequencing Processes to Eliminate Building in Batches

The simple task of examining and reorganizing the location of the equipment in your facility can lead your Teams to Mistake-Proofing solutions while at the same time increasing efficiency. In one factory that was manufacturing sensors, the simple act of diagramming the flow of the product through the facility revealed a ridiculously circuitous route for one product series. The equipment had been used to manufacture a type of sensor that had become obsolete and was no longer manufactured. However, it never occurred to anybody to combine all the equipment for the new sensor in one area to eliminate queue time, travel time, and batch building. Because of the Mistake-Proofing Team's work, the equipment was moved into one cell, reducing inventory and improving velocity and quality. If a process goes out of control, building in batches lends itself to accumulating multiple defects that go undiscovered until the item is put to use in the next stage of assembly. When a part is immediately put to use in the next stage of assembly, an error that is detectable at this stage is detected quickly before many more defective parts are manufactured. The defect creating process can be corrected quickly, preventing the creation of further defects. Again, Mistake-Proofing Teams should continue to look for a higher level Mistake-Proofing solution that will completely eliminate the possibility of an error occurring. Your manufacturing cells should always be under review for improvement.

Film Processing

A Team of Manufacturing Engineering folks were consolidating and improving a film-winding business in Connecticut from one location in Germany and another in California. Again, this was a medical imaging film product used in the cardio-vascular arena. The short version is this: we purchased very large rolls of film in large quantity and converted them into very small rolls of film (the winding operation), then packaged the film for customers to use in a hospital environment, shipping the film with the appropriate developer. The work had to be done in total darkness, no light whatsoever, and in a cool, dry environment. There were five winding rooms in California and one in Germany. After the move to Connecticut, the entire operation was accomplished in one efficient mistake-proofed winding room as described below.

- A revolving door that did not allow any light to enter permitted the operators to come and go without having to shut the operation down. Previously the individual rooms had to be shut down, and the product had to be sealed away to protect it from the light when the door was opened to permit entry and exit for any reason. Whenever an operator failed to seal a roll of very expensive film from exposure to light, the expensive film had to be scrapped.

- Another form of Mistake Proofing was accomplished by installing interlocking feeding doors to allow raw film to be fed into the room on one side and finished product to be passed out of the room on the other side, again permitting continuous operation when bringing material into and removing material from the room. The interlocking mechanism prevented doors being opened at the same time, eliminating the possibility of damaging light entering.

- Automatic cutters were installed on the rolling equipment, making this operation easy to perform in total darkness and eliminating the possibility of human error.

There were other innovative changes that made the winding tasks easier to perform in the dark. The Team involved with this transition had a lot of fun with this very successful Mistake-Proofing project. Long after the room was up and running in full production, the Team continued to make innovative Mistake-Proofing improvements with equipment and methods.

Eliminating Handling

Eliminating handling steps in the manufacturing process eliminates opportunities for errors at each of those eliminated steps. One Mistake-Proofing Team example took place in the sensor-manufacturing cell in a Connecticut factory where changing the type of epoxy used in the manufacturing process led to significant improvements. Epoxies that are cured with an ultraviolet light replaced time and temperature-cured epoxies that had to stand overnight to cure. UV cured epoxy allows the operator to cure the epoxy immediately after application with a hand-held ultraviolet light. The assembly process can continue without the need to rack, stack, and wait for the assembly to cure. This eliminates many touches as well as removing the curing queue time from the manufacturing cycle time. Also the new epoxies were able to be purchased premixed from the manufacturer. Buying them premixed eliminated the variability in the in-house mixing operation. Many types of epoxies are available premixed, packed in dry ice, and that can be shipped overnight. Usually this is an insignificant part of product cost, and the increased cost to buy premixed material is usually well worth the elimination of the variations in the mixing process. It also eliminates a job almost nobody likes.

Oil Leaks

One great example of a problem addressed by a final assembly Mistake-Proofing Team was X-ray housing oil leaks. The X-ray producing rotating anode device was sealed in a glass envelope. This tube, as it was called, was assembled into a leaded metal housing that was then filled with oil for cooling purposes. The metal sections had O-ring grooves machined in them, and the O-ring seals prevented the oil from leaking out. After the tubes were assembled, they would be tested with high power levels. This test produced a considerable amount of heat. It was at this stage that the oil leaks were detected. These oil leak problems persisted for years, despite a great deal of attention by Manufacturing, Engineering, and Quality Control personnel. Machined surfaces were improved, O-ring materials were changed, O-rings were soaked in oil for days prior to being used, and rigid specifications were imposed, but most of the oil leaks persisted. The oil leaks persisted until the Final Assembly Department Mistake-Proofing Team took on the problem.

The Team reviewed the problems carefully using the problem-solving techniques it had learned in the classroom and on the Shop Floor. Before long the Team had solved this serious problem. The solution had eluded our best engineers. In the process of assembling the metal-to-metal sections with the O-ring in between, the operator applied petroleum jelly to the O-ring before placing it in the O-ring groove. The assembly specification did not specify how much petroleum jelly to use; therefore, some operators used more than others. Some operators, believing that more is better, applied gobs of petroleum jelly. When the housing was heated during a test, the petroleum jelly turned to a liquid and gave the appearance of an oil leak. Since the oil used in the housing was virtually identical in appearance to petroleum jelly in a liquid state, the housing was deemed to be a "leaker," and the unit was disassembled and reworked at great expense.

The Pilot Team figured out what was happening. After all, they were the people closest to the operation, so it follows that with the proper training and motivation, they should be the people best qualified to resolve the problem. In this case, as in so many cases, the problem was not what it appeared to be; the housing was not leaking oil from inside. The immediate Mistake-Proofing solution was simply to correct the work instructions by specifying a light coating of petroleum jelly. The results turned in by the Team in solving this oil leak problem amounted to an 85 percent reduction in oil leaks and more than paid for the entire Mistake-Proofing Team training program for years to come.

Transaction Simplification

There were plenty of opportunities for the Teams to simplify the business transactions of transferring inventory from our vendor's inventory to our inventory. This was done electronically, using a barcode reader setting up the Accounts Receivable for the Vendor and Accounts Payable for us automatically when material ownership was automatically transferred to our possession. The material was then transacted out of our inventory when the finished item was transacted to final stock with a barcode wand, using the "backflushing" method based on our bills-of-materials. Our system knew what parts and how many were used to build a finished product; it was a simple process to have our business system deduct all these parts whenever we transacted a finished product to the finished goods stockroom from production. With this system, most of our material movement transactions were done electronically, eliminating the hundreds of errors normally created when thousands of items were keyed into the system by hand. Purchase Orders were not necessary; a simple letter of agreement with the Vendor covered each item. However, if you find it necessary to use Purchase Orders, the Purchase Orders can be created automatically with the signal to fill a requirement or as the requirement is being filled. At the same time the Accounts Receivable for the Vendor and Accounts Payable for your Company can be set up. The Purchase Order can be opened and closed simultaneously when the requirement is filled. This also works well for consignment inventory.

Dedicated Equipment Eliminating Setups

In this case the Team added an ultrasonic welder to a work cell, which eliminated an operator carrying work across the factory to an ultrasonic welder in another work cell, necessitating a change in setup and the waste of material in adjusting for the new setup. Again, eliminating the need to manufacture in batches and making the parts as they were needed made detecting errors quick so they could be corrected immediately and not after a large batch of defective parts were queued up for production. With the welder right in the cell where the assemblies were consumed, there was no need to change the equipment setup. The parts quality was consistently good, and with preventative maintenance it remained good.

Customers Ordering Their Own Products Using the Internet

This Team's Mistake Proofing was the result of an e-business campaign in Milwaukee. The decision was made to take product information to the next stage and allow Customers to place product orders over the

Internet, eliminating errors caused by internal order takers through misinterpreting the Customer's requirements. Customers were able to order simple products straight from the system or configure complex products online. In the latter instance, this service saved Sales staff many hours of face time working out order details with the Customers. If the sale was for a complex product with many different options and some of the options were not available on certain models, the automated ordering system was programmed to avoid any ordering errors matching features with models that a Salesman might make. Customers were even willing to work out delivery and installation times based on an availability schedule posted and automatically updated on the 'Net. Many Customers actually preferred to do their own ordering over the Internet, especially for more complex products, even though they were fulfilling the role normally filled by the Salesman. They built their own product at their leisure without the pressure of a Salesman's pitch. Also, Customers who used the products and the supplies that went with them found it convenient to order the supplies themselves. This service is especially convenient when they know exactly what they want and are ordering the same items over and over on a regular basis. They could order anytime at their convenience, twenty-four hours a day, seven days a week.

Original Equipment Manufacturers Monitor Your Equipment for Optimum Performance

 Our Teams found another fascinating use of the Internet as a tool is its application in diagnostics. Customers dialed into an equipment service center, hooked up a problem piece of equipment, and a service technician diagnosed and fixed the problem live in minutes. On one occasion one of our technicians was able to enhance the resolution of an image. This enhancement was credited with helping the doctors save the life of a child. The service was offered with new products to attract new business and was also sold separately with a service contract, generating another revenue stream.

 Large equipment manufacturers are marketing this service as another source of revenue, charging a fee for improving their Customers' efficiency. The equipment can be monitored twenty-four hours a day, and adjustments can be made while the equipment is running. These techniques are being applied to locomotives and jet engines. Imagine being able to monitor and tweak the equipment you build and supply remotely so that it always performs error free. Just being able to determine when a Customer's piece of equipment needs to be serviced to keep it performing at an optimum level, delivering error-free results, can bring a fortune in revenue. What a great Mistake-Proofing opportunity for your Teams to work with!

Component Manufacturers' Database Interacts with Your Design Software

Our Design Engineers had access to a vendor's database over the Internet that helped to determine the most effective electronic component to use in a circuit. The component's functional characteristics, as well as its footprint, could be quickly ascertained using the supplier's database. Some design systems can incorporate this data automatically, preventing design errors from occurring. One nice feature about these vendor sites is that many of them are available twenty-four hours a day, seven days a week. An Engineer working on a design at 9:00 p.m. in the evening does not have to wait until 8:00 a.m. the next day to sort out his technical issues with the supplier.

Pick and Pack

A Mistake-Proofing Team at a consumer products Company shipping to thousands of stores in the United States was picking and packing orders in a huge 500,000-square foot warehouse. Each order could call for any of 1,500 different items. One group of operators would pick the items, counting the ordered quantities out of bins containing the various products and placing the items in corrugated containers. Another group of checkers would remove the items packed and repack them to be sure the correct items and the correct quantities were present to fill the order. Double work to ensure the customer got what he or she ordered—the result of several customer complaints. The solution: insert a scale on the conveyor carrying the packaged items to the sealing station. The scale would weigh each carton, and the actual weight would be compared with the calculated weight. The calculated weight would be the sum of all the items in the order passing over the scale, traveling in sequence down the conveyor. All the items' weights were known to the business system and the total weight could be easily calculated. If by chance, an order's actual weight and the calculated weight differed, the carton would be moved off to a checking station where it could be checked and corrected. Thus, there was only a need to check a few orders rather than every order. This resulted in a significant labor savings when the thousands of orders that were processed in this warehouse were considered.

Packaging Equipment

A Team in a Company that cooked and packaged a product could potentially transfer the dreaded salmonella bacteria from the raw product to the cooked product, contaminating the finished item, necessitating its destruction and causing costly facility shutdowns for sterilizations. The solution was to split the factory in half, separating each half with a doorless wall. No employee was permitted from one side to the other without proper sterilization. An oven that cooked the product was placed in the wall between the two sides of the facility. The product traveled in the oven from one side of the building to the other. Timers were used to ensure the product was thoroughly cooked and safe from salmonella bacteria before being taken out of the oven for packaging.

Over-Cooked Membranes

Very expensive membranes used in a manufacturing process were boiled as part of the manufacturing process. As luck would have it, one Friday afternoon someone forgot to shut down the equipment doing the boiling. The result: a nasty Monday morning surprise requiring a lot of rework—not exactly the way to start off one's work week. The Team solution: install timers to shut down the boiling process automatically. This was a much safer solution than a pledge never to forget again.

Mother and Baby

Picture a busy doctor with mothers on the maternity floor and newborns in the nursery and neonatal intensive care unit. The doctor needs up-to-the-minute information about a mother and her baby, and he is in radiology on another floor reviewing images with a radiologist or in his office across town or in his dining room at home. He is reluctant to rely on someone else's interpretations of the up-to-the-minute patient data for mother and baby, consisting of vital signs, blood test results and images he needs to make his urgent treatment decision. The Team solution: an information technology system that allows the doctor to access the needed information from virtually anywhere on any device (e.g., computer, PDA, Smartphone, etc.) connected to the Internet, eliminating the possibility of mistakes occurring in having someone else interpret and summarize the patient data, then conveying that information verbally.

The above examples clearly demonstrate that Mistake-Proofing Team opportunities and solutions come in all varieties and sizes. They can dramatically affect both the quality of our output and the quality of our lives in the workplace and beyond. In most cases the Mistake-Proofing solutions are simple. A few of the solutions are more complex to execute, but the technology is there waiting to be applied by your Teams. The important task is to recognize that the technology needs to be brought together with the Mistake-Proofing opportunity.

Laying Out the Program

So you have decided to go forward with your Mistake-Proofing program and you would like to know what the whole program might look like. Well, some possibilities are laid out below.

Select a Program Champion

The individual you select as the program Champion will lead both phases of the training effort. The first phase will entail training virtually all employees, the second phase will be the ongoing training of all new employees. The Champion should be an individual who is well respected by everyone at all levels of the organization with some training experience. Also, it would be desirable to select a Champion with an understanding of process improvement and the application of problem-solving techniques. Some Six Sigma training would be ideal but is not necessary.

Kickoff

Make a splash and have some fun with this one. Party, posters, and publicity are the order of the day. Whatever you do, get the message across that top Management supports this program. Also send the message that everyone will be involved—every employee will be involved. If you are using a Self-Directed

Team, it should lay out the program and be part of the kickoff.

The Training

The training includes the following sections:

- Introduction – Mistake Proofing is awareness training employing common-sense solutions to eliminate process errors through the use of warnings or by designing processes that completely eliminate the possibility of making a mistake.

- Defects and Costs – Zero mistakes make for happy customers, and happy customers make for prosperous businesses. Prosperous businesses make for more secure jobs. More secure jobs make for happy employees. Fewer errors lead to lower costs and a better competitive advantage. The further into the process it is before you discover a mistake, the more costly it is to fix.

- Understanding Process Errors – Mistakes are preventable. Look to the process to resolve mistakes, not to the employee. If you have repeated mistakes, chances are there is something wrong with the process, not the employee. Anyone properly trained should be able to execute a task well. Inspection will not catch all mistakes.

- Two Levels of Mistake Proofing (Poka-yoke) – Low-Level Mistake Proofing will warn you that a mistake has just occurred or is about to occur. High-Level Mistake Proofing creates a process that makes it virtually impossible to make a mistake with the process. A simple example is the four-drawer file cabinet. At first there was no Mistake Proofing, and you could open more than one drawer at a time. If you opened two drawers at once, there was a good chance the file cabinet would fall forward, possibly causing injury. The first attempt at Mistake Proofing was to put a warning message on the front of the file drawers, warning not to open more than one drawer at a time. This was Lower-level Mistake Proofing. Nothing prevented someone from ignoring the message. The next attempt was to lock all the other drawers once a single drawer was opened insuring that you couldn't open more than one drawer at a time. This was Higher-Level Mistake Proofing—the lock absolutely prevented a second drawer from being opened.

- Tools and Methods of Mistake Proofing – They are many and varied and depend only on the imagination of the individual.

A few examples are the shape of items, scales, vision systems, counting method, colors, check lists, instructions, barcoding, and comparative databases.

- Problem-Solving Tools – The Define, Measure, Analyze, Improve and Control tool; Failure Mode and Effects Analysis; Brainstorming; Cause and Effect Diagram.

The training encourages participant interaction in the following ways:

- Counting specific letters in a paragraph to prove that 100 percent inspection is ineffective.

- Requesting that the participants come up with a list for each of the following:

  - Why they think people make mistakes? Examples are poor designs, fatigue, misunderstanding, personal illness, poor methods, boredom, lack of training, and distraction.

  - Common Examples of Mistake Proofing – Childproof locks in the home and car, circuit breakers, refrigerator lights that automatically go out when the door is closed, automatic seat belts, smoke alarms that beep when the battery is low, three-pronged plugs, printers that signal low ink levels, automatic lights that come on after dark, electric eyes on doors

- Examples of Mistake Proofing at work – These would depend on the type of business you are in

- The kind of errors that could occur in their area of work. *This is probably the most important part of the session.* This is where the participants will identify the things that irritate them in their day-to-day activities—the mistakes that happen over and over and never seem to go away. These are the mistakes that are stepped over. Many of these will surprise Management, and Management must react positively. If the employees identify problems and want to fix them, let them, and support their effort. Of course, you will want to set up an individual or group of individuals to pass on all the ideas your employees come up with. You don't want all your employees going off and changing processes without some oversight.

Remember their way may not be your way; however, you should consider that if they do it their way, they will be highly motivated to make it work—after all, it was their idea. They surfaced the problem and came up with the fix.

- Examples of lower-level Mistake Proofing – Color coding, warning messages, alarms, work instructions, and scales.

- Examples of higher-level Mistake Proofing – Barcoding, comparative database, alpha-numeric data checkers, photo eye, shape of a three-pronged plug. It is important that there be an understanding of the difference between a Lower-Level and an Upper-Level Mistake-Proofing solution because the work is never done until an economical Upper-Level solution is found.

When trying to come up with a Mistake-Proofing solution, the participants should consider the following:

- Define the problem.

- Measure the effects of the problem, including the cost.

- Identify the root cause of the problem.
- Find the best Mistake-Proofing method.
- Implement the method.
- Measure the results, and establish a method to monitor the results.
- Present your Mistake-Proofing opportunity and solution.

Request the participants break out into small Cross-Functional Teams ideally from different areas of the organization and work on Mistake Proofing the process problems they previously identified could occur in their area of work. The next day have the Teams return to the class with flip charts detailing three things—the item they selected to Mistake Proof, how it will be Mistake Proofed, and what the annual savings will be. After presented, each Team should commit to a date the project will be completed. If a project cannot be completed in less than two months, it is not right for this venue and should be tackled with a Self-Directed Team approach—see the chapter on Self-Directed Teams. Most Mistake-Proofing projects will be completed in one to two weeks, many in less than a few days. Initially, the solutions will be more Lower Level in nature than Higher Level. Over time, as the Teams' skills improve, the solutions will become more Higher Level.

Talk Up the Program—Posters, Newsletters, etc.

Giving the Mistake-Proofing program some initial publicity and conveying ongoing results to the entire organization will further the cause. Use these tools to talk up the training so that by the time the trainees enter the classroom they will be eagerly anticipating the fun. Yes, the fun. They will enjoy the change of pace that will give them a measure of control over solving their everyday work problems, some for the first time. Your employees will feel more valuable and valued while you will be giving them the most empowering gift of all, knowledge!

Reward Good Work, Give Recognition and Celebrate Success

A rewards plan will be immensely helpful in gaining support for the program. It should be made clear at the outset that the rewards are not an attempt to compensate the Teams for their ideas and hard work. They are merely an expression of gratitude and recognition. The reward can be a small gift certificate or dinner for two or a nice cash award, depending on the level of contribution. One Company I consulted for with several locations did something different in each location. In one location they gave a $50 gift certificate for each idea implemented. Another gave employees a day off if their idea was used. Yet another gave a cash award that varied depending on the value of the contribution.

Recognition is a very important part of the reward system, and for many, more important than any monetary gift. It costs the Company virtually nothing to recognize employee contributions, yet so many companies fail in this area. The program newsletter or area posters can be used to recognize contributors. Also, celebrations like pizza parties, Company luncheons, and picnics serve as good recognition occasions. All employee meetings and Companywide e-mails can serve to get the word out.

Don't forget to celebrate the program kickoff and major successes along the way. It can be as simple as cake and coffee or as elaborate as a formal party. Use your imagination or, better yet, let your Teams use their imaginations.

Tracking Performance

All successes should be quantified and reported into a central point. The results should be published for all to see. Management can use this information as the basis for making awards and giving recognition. The savings can be impressive, and the quality improvements can be great. Collect the data, and share the good news.

Chapter 5

Chapter 5

The Workout Team Process

The Workout Process combines the change acceleration process and gap analysis to arrive at a go forward consensus plan that can be quickly put in motion to achieve a desired result. We have used this approach to put in place a plan to implement a division-wide "enterprise resource planning" business system; resolve conflicts between senior Managers; develop strategic business plans to rescue failing businesses; dramatically remove costs from individual areas of businesses; restructure and reform trouble business functions within organizations; reduce millions in the costs of goods and services; and, after hurricane Katrina, we used this technique to develop a plan to quickly ramp up production of hydrogen in the Northeast as much of the nation's hydrogen production facilities were under water. Hydrogen is necessary for manufacturing metals, cooling gas turbines in power plants, and powering fuel cells, as well as many other applications. Hydrogen is a necessity without practical substitutes.

The Team's objective is to come up with a *consensus plan* that contains action steps, an action owner assigned to each action step, with a timeline commitment that when executed well will lead to a successful outcome. It is necessary for the Team first to define the *current state*—the actual conditions right now, today, so that everyone involved in the Workout has the same understanding of where you are starting from. The next step is to define the *desired state*, or future state where you want to end up after the consensus plan is executed.

Select the Facilitator carefully. He or she should be someone who is a well-respected person in the organization or someone from outside the business who has had experience facilitating this type of process. Holding the session off site is preferable to limit the possibility of interruptions and keep the group focused. It is recommended that flip charts be used to record the current state. Hang the flip charts on the wall for reference. When moving from the current state to defining the desired state, do the same thing—use flip charts to record the items and hang them on an opposing wall. To build a consensus plan, the Team will consider the actions necessary to move from the current state to the desired state. Brainstorming is a particularly helpful process for coming up with actions required to achieve the desired state. The Team records the action steps necessary to achieve the desired state and assigns responsibility and commitment dates to each of the action items. Only high-level action steps are necessary during the actual Workout. After the Workout session the action steps can be expanded to come up with a detailed action plan for each element of the consensus plan. A "risk analysis" should be conducted by the Team to identify potential risks with the consensus plans. Steps to mitigate each serious risk identified should be taken.

The techniques for running a Workout are simple and easy to understand and can be mastered relatively quickly. This simplicity makes this tool ideal for any size business or any size business problem that fits the circumstances best served by this process.

The first step in the process is to define the "current state." That is the way things really are right now. If the Team's goal is to develop a strategic business plan, you must first define the current state of the business. All Team members involved in the Workout should agree to what the current state of the business actually is. The current state can be defined in terms of numbers, organization charts, process maps, or any other device that conveys the current state of the business. Revenue, net profit, margin, bank-line performance, growth rates, budget performance, and other financial data will be helpful. Compensation plan, inventory analysis, ranking talent levels, customer service level, current markets served, quality of product/service, competition, product life cycles, existing cost-savings programs, an analysis of the technology and systems used in the business, including the use of the Internet, process issues, sales promotions and advertising, prevailing morale, and current vision statement. Add to the foregoing anything that helps define the current condition of the business.

It is *not* absolutely necessary to have each item defined to the last penny or last letter; however, it is important that information be at least directionally correct. Information can be further corroborated after the initial Workout by the Team to work out each detail. Remember, we are trying to put together an action plan that every Team member involved agrees to so that we can move forward. Part of the Team's consensus plan can be further defining some assumptions used to develop the plan. If the Team waits until it collects every last bit of data, it may end up doing nothing.

Once the Team has defined the current state of the business, and it is the general consensus of the group, members can move on to define the "desired state." What do they want the business to look like in the future? To do this, the Team can refer to the way it defined the current state for hints of areas that need or could use improvement. Add to this any other changes that would be an improvement in the business. The Team might, for example, want to increase the top and bottom line performance and/or the level of Management talent. Make these things part of your "desired state" definition. When all agree on the "desired state" definition, the Team can move on to building the consensus action plan with action owners and timeline commitments.

I suggest that the Team use some type of software that will track the progress you are making toward meeting your goal. I personally like Microsoft Project. Project lets you link dependent tasks, allowing you to readily see the effects of falling behind on a related task. The Team can also keep track of required resources. The software is pretty friendly and easily mastered.

In the above example of constructing a business plan, the Company's Team was able to put together a consensus plan that led to new, realistic, achievable financial goals, store closings in unprofitable locations, new store openings in profitable locations, a plan to upgrade employee talent, just to name a few of the actions that came out of this effort that took only a few days.

Other Examples of Successful Workouts

Implement a Division-wide Enterprise Resource Planning System

This business was a division of a major corporation that had dozens of different business systems. The business systems were inherited when other companies were acquired and merged into the Division. This made intercompany transactions difficult. You can imagine what rolling up the financials from dozens of different business systems at the end of month looked like. The Workout Team involved seven people who came up with a high-level consensus plan that moved this business to one business system that works very efficiently to this day. This plan was developed in less than one day. Of course, the Workout process was second nature to the Management in this business—it was used regularly to develop actionable plans by this Team.

Resolve Conflicts between Senior Managers

This process can be used to resolve conflicts between members of Management. By its nature, the process of putting together a consensus plan drives the Team players to work together to reach a common goal. Together they define the "current state," come up with the "desired state," and then create a consensus plan to arrive at the "desired state." This is a great way to get your people to work together.

Reduce the Cost of Goods and Services by $5 Million

This Workout took place in Washington State. When we arrived, the goal for cost savings was $500,000 for the next year. When asked what and how the savings were to be achieved, no one had any answers. A formal plan was a foreign concept to this group. Three days later, after a Workout involving a Cross-Functional Team of employees, the Company had a consensus plan to save millions of dollars. The plan identified just how the savings were to be achieved with individuals signed up for each task with a timeline commitment. Members of the Team raised their hands and made commitments to one another. Vendors were identified, redesigns were committed to, plans were made to bring some items in-house as well as subcontract other items outside that were done in-house, and material substitutions were suggested for review. Actual savings for the following year amounted to over $5,000,000.

Packaging Issues Resolved

This Company in New Jersey had many serious packaging issues that went unresolved. Finger pointing was the order of the day in this organization. The solution: get all involved in a Workout. This Workout Team involved over twenty people—a larger group than normal. At the start of the session, everyone was pointing at one another. Everything that was wrong with packaging in this Company was someone else's fault. After the first few hours, everyone involved realized there was not an innocent player in the room. All had contributed to the problem in some way. The session was cathartic. Only after everyone on the Team had a clear understanding of the "current state" could they move on and solve the packaging problems—which they were then able to do.

Chapter 6

Chapter 6

Problem-Solving Tools and Techniques

Problem-solving tools and techniques are an important part of any Team effort. As you will have a variety of talent involved in your Team activities, keep the tools and techniques in your training simple and easy to understand.

Cause-and-Effect Diagram

The cause-and-effect diagram (sometimes called the fish-bone diagram) is very effective yet easy to understand. An example is below:

Cause and Effect Diagram (Fishbone)

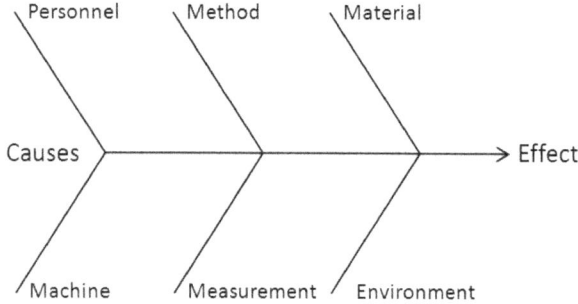

The effect is placed at the head of the arrow, and all the possible causes are listed on the legs of the diagram. Each possible cause is then analyzed to determine its contribution to the effect. This technique is easy to use and easy to understand.

Failure Mode and Effects Analysis

This tool is also simple to use and understand. It takes only a little practice to become fond of the Failure Mode and Effects Analysis tool. See the example below:

FMEA

Failure Mode and Effects Analysis

Problem	Consequence	Frequency	Severity	Detection	Score
Wrong amount	Short pay	1	8	2	**16**
Wrong date	Pay late	2	5	5	50
Wrong address	Never pay	4	10	10	400

In the first column, list the problem. On the first line in this example, the problem is invoicing for the wrong amount. The second column lists consequences. The consequence of invoicing for the wrong amount is being paid short. The third column lists the frequency of invoicing for the wrong amount. On a scale of one to ten, with one being the lowest, the frequency of this occurring is ranked as a one. In other words there is a one in ten chance of invoicing for the wrong amount and then being paid short. The fourth column indicates the severity of being paid short. On a scale of one to ten, with one being the lowest, the severity of being paid short is eight. In this case you could never be paid all of your money; hence the condition gets a rank of eight. The fifth column lists detection. On a scale of one to ten, with one being the lowest, the difficulty of detecting the invoicing problem is ranked as a two. There is a 20 percent chance that the invoice problem would be detected; therefore, it received a rank of two, as two is 20 percent of ten. To determine the score, simply multiply the Frequency times the Severity times the Detection and enter the result in the score column. In this case 1 X 8 X 2 = 16. Repeat this multiplication for the other problems identified, and list the results in order by score. Address the problems that get the highest score first. You may choose not to address problems that receive a very low score.

There are certain characteristics of a problem that would cause it to receive a low score. A very low rank for frequency, severity, or detection, such as a score of one, would result in a pretty low overall score. For instance, a rank of four for frequency, ten for severity, and one for detection would result in a total score of only forty because 4 X 10 X 1 = 40. In this example the problem is highly detectable so the consequences can be mitigated by detection; hence, a low score of forty. You will want to fix the problem in time, but it will probably not be your most pressing problem needing immediate attention. On the other hand, if detection had received a rank of ten—meaning that the problem is not detectable, the total score would have been four hundred because 4 X 10 X 10 = 400. The much higher score of four hundred requires immediate action. A high difficulty of detection rank of ten gives us a hint that part of a mitigating solution may be to come up with a method of detecting the problem before it can cause a severe problem.

This is an excellent tool to add to anyone's problem-solving tool box because it is easily explained and understood. Someone who has had little exposure to these types of tools may find using this technique a bit formidable at first. However, after the tool is used just a few times, almost anyone will become comfortable with failure mode and effects analysis, making it easy to identify and prioritize the most significant problems that could arise without the emotion that can often send you off in the wrong direction.

Brainstorming

Brainstorming is an excellent method of coming up with solutions to problems. To get my point across, I have often said that I have never met an individual who is smarter than ten dumb people in a room, and I know a lot of very smart people. You may think this statement is a bit too dramatic; however, I would ask you to think about it before you jump to that conclusion. There is something kind of magical that happens when you get a group of people together to brainstorm. In a brainstorming session, someone throws out an idea. That idea spurs someone else in the group to get an idea that he or she never would have come up with had he or she not heard the idea previously thrown out. Multiply this times ten people, and the sum is truly greater than the whole. This is the power of brainstorming.

In a brainstorming session, a group of folks sit around a table and brainstorm for ideas.

As the ideas are brought up, they are recorded. Some groups use flip charts; other groups use file cards or record the ideas on a PC that is projected on a screen. I like to use flip charts for recording the ideas so that they can be taped to the walls for all participants to reference as the session progresses.

It is important that all ideas be respected, especially unpopular ideas—often the minority ideas bring with them the most effective solutions. After all, if the solutions were so obvious, why would the group need to hold a brainstorming session? The brainstorming should continue until either no more ideas are forthcoming or the ideas that are forthcoming are really dumb ones. At this point the brainstorming portion of the work is called complete by the brainstorming leader, and hopefully the best solution to the problem is apparent.

As it is likely that several different solutions emerge to the same problem, categorize them in a four-blocker like the one below.

4-Blocker

	High	Low
Easy	Easy with High Payoff	Easy with Low Payoff
Difficult	Difficult with High Payoff	Difficult with Low Payoff

Ease of Implementation (vertical axis) — *Payoff* (horizontal axis)

Ideas that are easy to execute with a high payoff go in the upper left quadrant. Ideas that are easy to implement but have a low payoff go in the upper right quadrant. Ideas that are difficult to implement with a high payoff go in the lower left quadrant. Finally, ideas that are difficult to execute with a low payoff go in the bottom right quadrant.

Next, pick the idea or combination of ideas that will give you the highest level solution to your Mistake-Proofing problem and that will be the least difficult to implement.

Six Sigma

Both Statistical Process Control (SPC) and Mistake Proofing (Poka-yoke) are Six Sigma tools, as are Failure Mode Effects Analysis (FMEA) and the other problem-solving tools. We have talked about each of these tools. Of course, each of these tools can be used separately and do not have to be part of a Six Sigma program. Many smaller organizations will shy away from a full-blown Six Sigma program, which can be expensive and difficult to implement. Six Sigma requires a much more complex infrastructure for training and a much larger resource commitment for support than does a Mistake-Proofing program. Sure, it would be nice if the resources were available for a full-blown Six Sigma program; however, much progress can be made using simpler tools such as Mistake Proofing. So if you are a smaller organization, start with a Mistake-Proofing program, and when you collect from the payoff of your efforts here move on to Six Sigma, but don't think for a minute that you cannot compete without it.

One point I would like to make here is Six Sigma quality level would be 3.4 failures per million opportunities while Shigeo Shingo's Poka-yoke methods say do not rest until there are zero defects. Which plane do you want to fly on?

"We Have No Data, But We Are Sure" in Connecticut

Just because we do not have a full-blown Six Sigma program in place does not mean that we do not use Six Sigma methodology to bring some level of structure to solving our problems.

I offer the following in support of the above statement:

I was asked by a friend to assist in one of his companies. The problem: complete product failures leading to a total product recall and total shutdown of the manufacturing facility. On my first visit I convened a meeting, bringing together about twenty of this Company's best and brightest. Virtually all were degreed engineers, and several had advanced degrees, including some with their PhDs. I was told that they were sure they knew what the problem was. The culprit was a sharp metal shard that was piercing a membrane, causing the equipment to short out and fail completely. At that point I said to myself, "Self, you will have this one licked and be out of here in less than five days," and of course I would be a hero with my friend. Well, things didn't quite go the way I thought they would at that moment. When I asked to see the data, I was told that they had no data, but they knew the problem was metal shards. I then asked the

Team to collect the data. I was told that this would take several days. We called the meeting and agreed to reconvene several days later when the field returns had been inspected and the data had been collected.

The Team reconvened several days later. At that time I was told that we did not have all the data yet; however, now the engineers were sure that sharp metal shards were less than 50 percent of the problem. I knew then that I would be with this Company for a while, and my daydream of delighting my friend with a speedy solution was lost. In fact, I spent the better part of ten months with this Company. In the end, sharp metal shards did not cause any of the failures. The real cause of the problem was torque pressure.

The approach that brought this Company back from the brink was simply to apply Six Sigma methodology in the broadest sense. I insisted that the Team follow the DMAIC method.

Define

Measure

Analyze

Improve

Control

Define the problem: in the shard case, defining the problem correctly would have gone a long way toward solving the problem, leading to a solution. Measure: collect and measure the data. Analyze: analyze the data collected. Improve: improve the process/product. Control: put controls in place to assure that the solution continues to be effective. The result was to bring structure to the Company's problem-solving approach.

The problem was identified, fixed, and mistake-proofed. The Company resumed manufacturing and successfully replaced all customer products that had failed.

These are only a few of the many problem-solving tools and techniques that can be used by your Teams. These were selected because they are particularly helpful, and they are also easy for the trainer to explain and easy for the trainee to understand. I encourage the Team to explore the use of other problem-solving tools and techniques. Meanwhile these will serve to get your Teams under way.

Chapter 7

Chapter 7

Team Dynamics

Understanding Team dynamics is important to the success of the Team. In each Team, people have varying roles, work habits, backgrounds of reference, skills, opinions, and personalities. These differences result in the Team not always agreeing. Performance is hindered when Teams do not work collaboratively together. In each Team there are many different components. Each Team develops its own entity. If the Team is effective, being a member of a Team can be a satisfying experience for all of the participants. The Team develops a sense of pride and shared accomplishment.

In order for a Team to be successful, there are key elements that must occur:

Helpful Hints for Team Success

- Team Goal – the Team must have a clearly defined goal. All members must understand why they are part of the Team and what the task at hand is. The goal could be broken into smaller, easier to understand pieces so it feels more attainable to the Team members.

- Team Rules – the Team must establish rules that hold members accountable for their meeting attendance. This should be done early in the Team forming process.

- Time Management – all Team meetings must begin and end on time. It is unfair to make those who arrive on time wait for late arrivals. Eventually, other Team members will come later, knowing that the meeting will not begin on time. Just starting the meeting on time with the Team members who show up on time will embarrass the members who walk in late. Timely starts should encourage more members to be on time in the future. If there are both set meeting start and end times, it is easier to keep the Team on task. The Team Leader or Facilitator should be responsible for keeping the

Team on task. Giving a five-minute warning allowing for a recap will be helpful. It is important to be respectful of the ending time since people have other meetings and obligations. By making time a priority, you are demonstrating that all members' time is valuable. If a meeting runs too long, members can easily become tired, distracted, and frustrated—Team productivity will decrease.

- Timelines – establishing timelines that include who will do what and by when are essential to successful Team performance. To ensure the timeline is being followed, a "check-in" (debriefing) should occur at the beginning of each meeting—this also adds a level of accountability. Use this "check-in" process to define what the Team is expected to accomplish by the end of the meeting. At the end of each meeting, the Team should review what it expects to be accomplished by the next meeting. Meeting times, dates, and locations should be established before the meeting ends.

- Team Size – Teams must have an appropriate size. Teams do not work well if they are too large or too small. If too large, the Team will be tough to manage, and consensus will be difficult to achieve.

If the Team is too small, you will sacrifice the benefits of drawing on organizational cross-functional talents. A Team with too few members will have fewer people to share the workload.

- Social Skills – Team members must possess moderate social skills and strong values that drive appropriate behavior.

- Resources – Teams must have the resources and materials needed to accomplish the goal. It is important to anticipate the group's needs, such as computers, folders, binders, markers, flip charts, as well as access to information. If people need to bring resources or information, this should be made clear well before the meeting.

- Meeting Space – meeting space must be comfortable for the Team size and cool enough to keep everyone awake, yet not cold.

- Participation – participation of all group members is important for a successful Team. Each member should be allocated a responsibility that will contribute to the success of the project.

- Cohesion – a cohesive group will be able to accomplish more in a shorter amount of time. This process of cohesion keeps Team members connected and creates lasting bonds which will benefit the organization beyond meeting the current Team Goals.

- Set Boundaries – boundaries and ground rules must be established up front. This should be done early, preferably in the first meeting. All Team members should agree to the rules and commit to follow them.

- Active Listening – the Leader and/or Facilitator should be active listeners—frequently restating and summarizing the points to reinforce that everyone understood the points being made. This summary also gives group members validation of their ideas.

Team Pitfalls

Groups should avoid pitfalls when possible. It is important to know what possible pitfalls can occur so they can be identified early on and dealt with appropriately.

- Burnout – burnout is a Team problem that can occur when Team members take on more than they can handle. They often over commit and find it difficult to admit they are struggling and need help. This occurs most commonly when the Team has a deep desire to "look good" and accepts a goal that is too aggressive.

- Power Struggles – power struggles can often occur when an individual carries a disproportionate share of the work. They become so invested in the work that they find it difficult to share credit or allow their work to be tampered with by the other Team members.

- Groupthink – groupthink happens when the Team is unwilling or unable to consider alternative ideas or approaches. The Team lacks critical thinking and is unwilling to debate ideas. Groupthink can happen when Team Leaders overemphasize the importance of Team unity without emphasizing the need to surface the best ideas possible.

Skills of a Group Leader

A good Team Leader is important to the Team's success. In order for multiple perspectives to be applied to complex issues, the Leader must ensure there is inclusiveness, sensitivity to others, and tolerance. It is important for the Team Leader to understand group dynamics.

The Team Leader or Team Facilitator should monitor the group interaction. After the Team has met a few times, the Leader should allow time for reflection to discuss how the Team is going. He or she should ask questions to determine whether Team members feel they are on task and comfortable with the process. Also he or she should try to ascertain whether everyone clearly understands his or her roles. The Team's perceptions about the state of the group are important. Positive perceptions will help to ensure Team success.

An effective Leader gives direction to the discussion and keeps everyone focused on the task at hand. Without direction, the Team can wander aimlessly. An effective Leader will exert pressure, sometimes indirectly, to help the Team keep moving forward. A Leader understands the value of time and must work to limit extraneous and repetitious discussion. A recorder should be appointed to keep a written record of the Team's progress. This will also help keep the Team from returning to the same items that have been previously settled.

An effective Leader will create an environment where open and effective communication takes place. Developing a sense of trust within the Team will ensure Team members that their contributions, opinions, and views are valued and important. This trust will help the entire Team accept ownership of the

Team output, while fostering good Team communication and accountability.

A Team Leader would benefit from conflict resolution training. Conflict among Team members can be a good thing and is sometimes unavoidable. Constructive conflict is okay. Conflict is important and can be an opportunity for effective decision-making, accuracy, insight, understanding, trust, and innovation. Conflict can also provide an opportunity for open communication and creative thinking. Differences need to be dealt with directly and not avoided. If this is done as a Team, everyone's views can be heard and a consensus agreement reached that makes sense to everyone involved.

An effective Team Leader will maintain a positive atmosphere. The Leader and or Facilitator must observe and be aware of how members are participating and interacting. Care should be taken to observe body language and other nonverbal communications of Team members.

The following is a list of suggestions of what leaders can say to promote clarity and keep the discussion moving in a Team setting:

- Here is my understanding…
- What if we…?
- What else…?
- Let's just listen to all the ideas and then see what makes the most sense…

- What do people think about…?
- Let's look at the pluses and minuses…
- Help me understand…
- Could you say more about…?
- Here are the areas where we are disagreeing…
- Let's identify…
- Here is what we seem to agree on…
- How about if we…?
- Let's spend a few more minutes…
- Maybe we should come back to this…
- Let's try to…
- Can we go back to…?
- We need to make a decision on this…
- Let's look at where we are…
- Are we ready to make a decision on…?
- Let's see where people stand on this…
- What do we already know…?
- What else do we need to find out…?

Suggested ground rules the Team Leader could introduce include the following:

- Team members do not interrupt each other. Even if you disagree with an idea, all must be allowed to state their ideas fully. Every Team member is entitled to his or her own opinion. Everyone has a chance to speak.

- Side discussions do not occur except between people working collaboratively on a project.

- Disagreements are okay. If an issue arises, it should be discussed.

- When a decision is reached, all members will support the decision.

- All members commits to their roles and participate fully—shared responsibility.

- Tolerance – Each person agrees to be respectful of others' roles, cultures, differences, value systems.

- Each person agrees to communicate openly and honestly.

- Each member agrees to attend all Team meetings and be on time.

- All meetings will begin and end on time.

- The Team agrees to stay on topic.

- A creative environment is supported with open-mindedness, which encourages risk taking. There are no bad ideas.

Intergroup Dynamics

Team dynamics are created by the relationships Team members have with each other. When people are working together, it's inevitable that they will have influence on plan one another. Several dynamics can occur within the group:

- Group personalities – Many different personalities influence interactions within a group. It is possible that at times there will be personality clashes. Some may perceive that the work is not fairly distributed, or they may perceive that others are not as committed as they are. Often the most "powerful" member will take on too many of the group's responsibilities and thus face the possibility of "burnout." To prevent both of these issues from occurring, the Team Leader can encourage the Team to distribute the work more evenly among the members.

Other personality traits that can affect a Team include the following:

- A shy person is likely to sit back in a group and be passive.

- An impatient person is likely to push the discussion ahead, even if things are not fully discussed.

- A confident person will offer more opinions.

- Power seekers may look for flaws in other Team members' work.

- Domineering personalities often want to take over the Team and often will resort to intimidation tactics (either consciously or unconsciously).

- Some people working on a Team unconsciously perceive the situation as competitive. This perception can lead to competitive feelings and generate behavior that can become destructive and harmful to the Team. People can perceive disagreements with ideas as "put-downs." These Team members may try to protect themselves and try to sabotage the ideas of those who disagreed with them.

- When Team members have different communication styles, they may frequently misunderstand one another. What sounds like an order to one person may be meant only as a suggestion.

- Some members may dominate Team meetings unintentionally. This may cause other participants to become resentful. The Leader can determine the Team's reaction by observing the facial expressions and body language (non-verbal communication) of the other participants when the dominant member starts speaking.

- Problems can occur when creative ideas and input from individual members are claimed by others on the Team. It should be emphasized that Team efforts belong to the Team. Resentment can occur if someone claims or gets individual credit.

- Conformity without exploring all possible options occurs when individuals on a Team want to conform too easily to establish a consensus. Conformity happens for a number of reasons, including the needs to feel liked, respected, and valued. People will censor their own ideas according to what they believe the Team wants to hear. Idea agreement can be gained too quickly in a Team setting before all the possibilities are adequately explored.

- "Groupshift" occurs when the positions individuals would normally take as non-team members are exaggerated toward more extreme positions because of their Team membership.

- Norms are the informal rules adopted by the Team to regulate members' behavior. Norms refer to what members believe "should be done" and represent value judgments about what is considered an appropriate behavior in various situations. These norms are usually not written down or even discussed, but they have a powerful influence on group behavior.

- "Scapegoating" occurs when Team members are singled out to take blame or unwarranted treatment. Scapegoating may be conducted against individuals or a group of people.

- The perception of "in" and "out" groups—or favoritism—occurs when people have preferences within the Team. Some are perceived to be in the "in" group, and the "out" group are those who feel outside of the "in" group.

Having a good understanding of the Team dynamics presented here will help Team Leaders and Facilitators manage their Teams to achieve greater success.

EPILOGUE: A FINAL WORD

Don't just put this book down and go back to doing business as usual.

- *Take a look at your business.*
- *Compare your Teams to the ones described in this book.*
- *Get your employees involved in converting your business into a lean, money-making enterprise by employing the Team concepts described in this book.*

Actions say more than words, and your words must be backed by actions. Your Company can achieve great results. Your employees can do it for you. Just ask them—they are ready to help.

Sources

Buckley, Ronald L. and Lucinda A. Buckley, *Lean Business Drivers,* Norwalk, CT: Shady Brook Press, 2012.

Buckley, Ronald L. and Lucinda A. Buckley, *My Toaster's Grandfather,* Norwalk, CT: Shady Brook Press 2012.

Buckley, Ronald L. and Candace-Lynn Buckley, *No Eraser Needed: Mistake Proofing Your Business*, Clifton, NJ: Sax Macy Fromm, 2012.

Buckley, Ronald L., *Winning in a Highly Competitive Manufacturing Environment,* Norwalk, CT: Shady Brook Press, 2003.

Buckley, Ronald L. and Lucinda A. Buckley, *Winning Manufacturing Solutions,* Norwalk, CT: Shady Brook Press, 2012.

Galsworth, Gwendolyn D., *The Visual Systems: Harnessing the Power of a Visual Workplace*, New York: AMACOM/American Management Association, 1997.

Katzenbach, Jon R. and Smith, Douglas K., *The Wisdom of Teams: Creating the High-Performance Organization,* New York: Harper Business Essentials, 1994.

Pande, Peter S., Neuman, Robert P. and Cavanagh, Roland R., *The Six Sigma Way,* New York: McGraw-Hill Company, 2000.

Schonberger, Richard J., *World Class Manufacturing: The Next Decade, Building Power, Strength, and Value,* New York: The Free Press, 1996.

Shigeo Shingo, *Zero Quality Control: Source Inspection and the Poka-yoke System,* Stamford, CT and Cambridge, MA: Productivity Press, 1986.

Wiig, John H., *Fix That Business,* John H. Wiig, 2012.

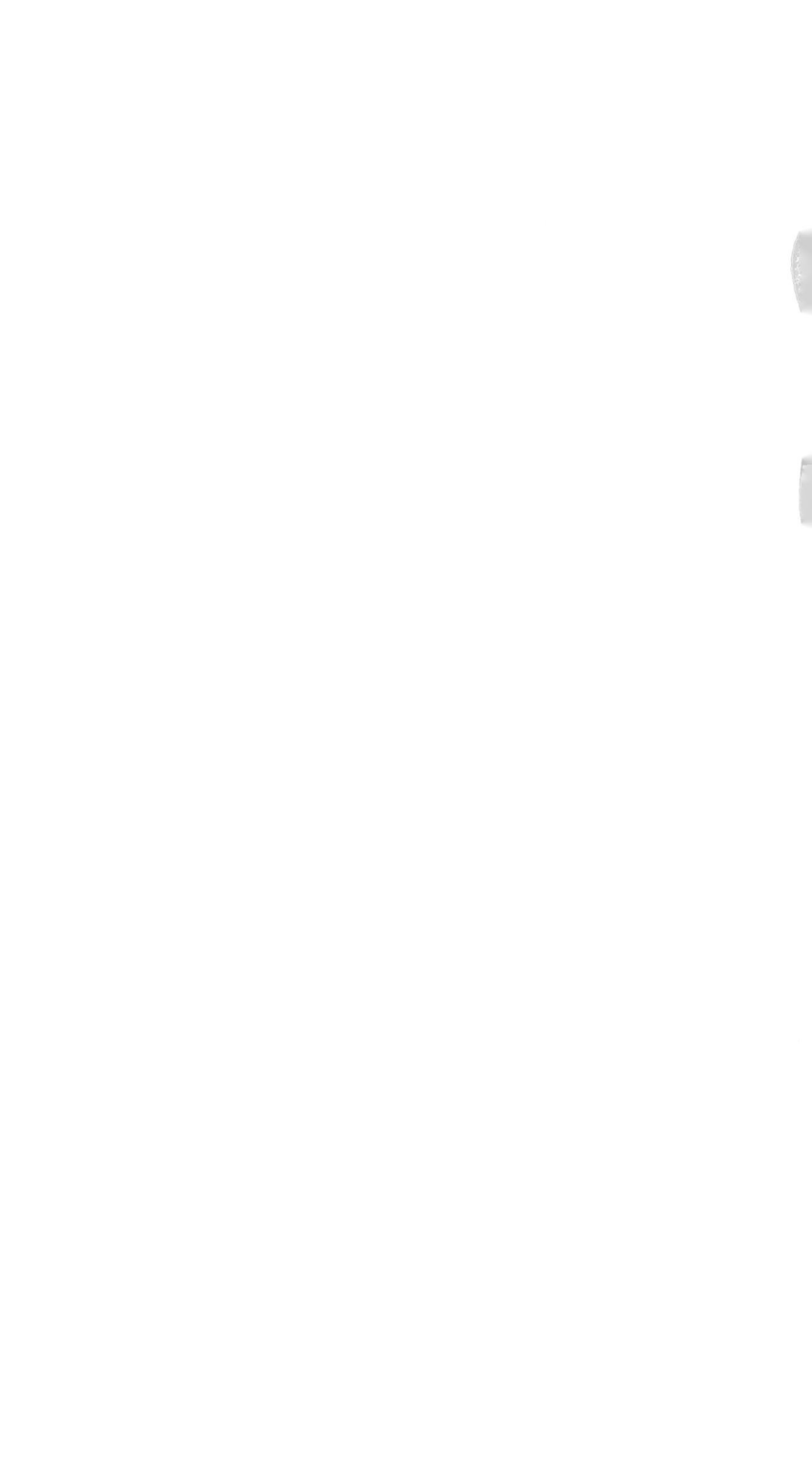

www.ingramcontent.com/pod-product-compliance
Lightning Source LLC
Chambersburg PA
CBHW061509180526
45171CB00001B/109